From the reviews of
Fires in the Bathroom:
Advice to Teachers from High School Students
(Also available from The New Press)

Fires in the Middle School Bathroom

Fires in the
Middle School Bathroom

Advice for Teachers from Middle Schoolers

Kathleen Cushman

Laura Rogers, EdD

THE NEW PRESS

NEW YORK
LONDON

Generous support from the MetLife Foundation made possible the research and writing of this book. It was written for What Kids Can Do, Inc. (WKCD), a national nonprofit organization based in Providence, Rhode Island, which aims to bring forward the voices of youth on issues that matter in their lives, learning, and work. For more information, see www.whatkidscando.org.

First published in the United States by The New Press, New York, 2008
This paperback edition published by The New Press, New York, 2009
Distributed by Perseus Distribution

LIBRARY OF CONGRESS CATALOGING-IN-PUBLICATION DATA

Cushman, Kathleen.
  Fires in the middle school bathroom : advice for teachers from middle schoolers / by Kathleen Cushman and Laura Rogers.
      p   cm.
  Includes bibliographical references and index.
  ISBN 978-1-59558-111-2 (hc)
  ISBN 978-1-59558-483-0 (pb)
    1. Middle school teaching—United States. 2. Middle school students—United States—Attitudes.   I. Rogers, Laura.   II. Title.
  LB1623.5.C88   2007
  373.236—dc22   2007047177

The New Press was established in 1990 as a not-for-profit alternative to the large, commercial publishing houses currently dominating the book publishing industry. The New Press operates in the public interest rather than for private gain, and is committed to publishing, in innovative ways, works of educational, cultural, and community value that are often deemed insufficiently profitable.

www.thenewpress.com

Composition by dix!
Photographs of students by Kathleen Cushman

Printed in the United States of America

10   9   8   7   6

This book is dedicated

to Ted and Nancy Sizer

and to

all the teachers who are listening

and all the students waiting to be heard

Contents

Preface

This book came about because of the wide interest sparked among educators by its 2003 predecessor, *Fires in the Bathroom: Advice to Teachers from High School Students*, by Kathleen Cushman. In that volume, students from four urban areas around the United States offered their perspectives on classroom teaching and learning, along with suggestions for increasing their motivation and engagement in school. Like this book, *Fires in the Bathroom* took shape with the support of the MetLife Foundation, whose Supporting New Teachers Initiative recognizes how much teachers can learn from students, if only given the chance. What Kids Can Do, a small nonprofit organization aimed at raising youth voices on issues that matter, sponsored the research and writing of both books.

Although *Fires in the Bathroom* was intended for an audience of new teachers in urban high schools, educators and students in many other settings responded to the candid, astute voices of its student co-authors. Their observations may have originated in big-city public high schools, but they also struck a deep chord with teachers in suburban, rural, and independent schools.

Teachers of the middle grades responded, too, especially those new to the profession. Like their high school counterparts, they sometimes found themselves wondering what to do when, as one high school student put it in the first book, "she's trying to be so nice and they're setting fires in the bathroom." These teachers read the advice of high school students with great interest, but also with caution. Their middle school students might care just as much about many of the issues high schoolers raised, but they seemed to care in a different way. When teachers discovered fires in the *middle school* bathroom, they noted, those fires were almost certainly lighted in a very different frame of mind.

These middle-grades teachers had their own questions for younger students: What helps you want to try hard in school—or keeps you from doing so? How can we help you deal with the social issues and pressures you face? What's fair in the classroom, and why? What helps you understand your challenging academic subjects? When it comes to your parents, what do teachers need to know and do? How can we best prepare you for the transition to high school?

In summer and fall 2005, Kathleen Cushman traveled to five urban areas (Rhode Island, California, New York, Indiana, and Connecticut) to record the thoughts and suggestions of forty urban middle schoolers from over a dozen schools. Some spent a few hours in those sessions, others a few days. The differences in their responses—some terse and guarded, others loquacious and opinionated—reflected not just the length of time they spent in dialogue, but also variations in their ages and grades, the schools they attended, and the backgrounds from which they came. Every conversation yielded new questions, and often surprising answers. (When students spoke in nonstandard English, we left their language unedited.)

Laura Rogers joined this project as co-author to help distill and interpret the transcripts of the students' responses. A developmental psychologist and teacher educator, she brings thirty years of experience working with adolescents to the task of understanding student declarations that otherwise seemed wildly inconsistent. (She spent the past twelve of these years in a public charter school for students in grades seven through twelve, which together the two authors helped to start.) Her experience working with teachers brought us confidence in the book's purpose, methods, and structure (explained in our first chapter). Our own back-and-forth conversations about what the students were telling us helped us set their advice and admonitions into a developmental context. In doing so, we aim to help teachers gain new perspectives, sustain their good humor, and continue to develop in their profession.

We hope you will recognize the enormous importance you have to your students. When the students in this book talked about instruction, they largely talked about how they felt about their teachers, and how their teachers made them feel about themselves as learners. As you listen to them speak of their hopes and their vulnerabilities, we have confidence that you will find ways to better support them during their journey on the middle school bridge.

Kathleen Cushman and Laura Rogers
Harvard, Massachusetts
July 2007

Fires in the Middle School Bathroom

Introduction: Journey over a Bridge

"Middle school still teaches you, but it's a part of growing up."

What do we mean when we say students are entering "middle school"? By the time they reach sixth, seventh, and eighth grades, students occupy a middle ground. They have gone beyond elementary schooling but they have not yet reached the high school years. They are experiencing rapid growth and change, in almost every way one can name. Depending on their school, they may find themselves in a building that includes kindergarten through grade eight, grades five or six through eight, or even grades six through twelve. These days, educators hotly debate the best way to arrange those grade levels. But whichever it is, the students feel in the middle of some big shift—an important passage from "little kid" to "almost grown up." These are their middle school years.

Middle schoolers (as we will refer to them here) know that they are facing big changes as they move up from the elementary to the middle grades—but they may not feel sure what to expect. They know they are growing up—but they don't know quite what that means, or how to do it.

Middle school is before you're an adult, but you're not a little kid anymore. You're not driving and you're not grown up.   RACHELL

First to fifth grade is more the basics, learning the subjects. When you go to middle school it's actually like a social-slash-learning place—you can talk and everything, but you get work. Middle school still teaches you, but it's a part of growing up. It's something you need to prepare for high school, a break in between, like a lunch break at work. Then in high school, you got more work.   KAITLYN

I think the only purpose of middle school is actually to prepare you for high school.   HEATHER

As a middle school teacher, you may feel a similar "in-between" uncertainty as you enter your classroom each day. Your job plainly requires that you teach students academic skills and content, preparing them for more difficult high school work. Yet you also have an even harder role to play. How can you best guide this varied group as they make the transition from childhood to young adulthood?

Students do not necessarily know the answer to that question. Even so, as they talk here about their middle school experiences, they draw a picture that can help you do your work well. They tell you where they are starting from, where they are heading, and how it feels to them along the way—providing crucial information to teachers and other adults in their lives.

Experienced teachers often tell us that it took them years to recognize that even if they are consistent and firm with their students, their students do not return the favor by acting consistently themselves. Your strategies may work one day, but they will not necessarily work the next. This book should help you understand why.

Twelve-year-old Katelin, for example, offers her best thinking on the subject of the playground conflicts that often draw her in. She declares:

> If you're getting ready to fight someone, it's better off that you go tell a teacher, so that you don't get in trouble for it and suspended.

Yet in the very next breath, she adds:

> But I don't think I would go. I would just fight that person.

Without skipping a beat, Katelin has turned from one perspective to another. How can her teacher work with that seeming contradiction? The answer lies in her words, no matter how illogical they might seem to us. By listening closely, we learn that Katelin is caught between competing claims: the childlike imperative to retaliate in kind collides with her growing appreciation of the expectations of her teachers and school community. On any particular day, Katelin is telling us, she might either get into the fight or report the problem to the teacher.

Over the long term, middle-grades teachers know they must provide clear expectations for Katelin's behavior so she will rise to those expectations. Day to day, however, teachers realize that firmness and consistency are not the only strategies they will need. They will also have to hear and respond to the dilemmas expressed in their students' contradictory words and actions.

Teachers of the middle grades must learn to recognize those dilemmas, while at the same time supporting students in learning to make better decisions. This book calls on students' own words to help teachers with that challenge.

Because the students are inconsistent in the way they frame their concerns and in what they ask of their teachers, we cannot simply accept their words as "advice for teachers" (as we did with older students' words in the 2003 book *Fires in the Bathroom: Advice for Teachers from High School Students*). Instead, we will place what middle-grades students say into the frame of early adolescent development.

Our young contributors are making their wobbly way across a bridge, with elementary school on one shore and high school on the other. Behind them lies the world of childhood, and they are inching toward another world where they will need to make sense of more complicated thoughts, feelings, and interactions. In the words of students like Katelin, we can see the developmental shifts that students make on that journey, and the unsteadiness that inevitably accompanies significant periods of change.

Every teacher of the middle grades will recognize the continual back-and-forth that students experience during this time:

- They want us to see them as more mature, but many of them still look like children.
- They want to be treated as more independent, serious young people, and they still want recess.
- They want to learn really interesting, "hard" things, but they want to learn them through games and activities.
- They want to be treated fairly—"just like everyone else"—and they also want us to make exceptions for them when they make mistakes.
- They want our recognition for what they do right, but they don't want anyone else to see us give it.
- They want to experiment with the rules—sneaking to the bathroom to

snack or play with fire—but they do so without guile, and so they get caught.

New middle school teachers who try to follow the advice of others—whether the advice comes from veteran teachers or from students like the ones in this book—will soon find themselves in impossible binds. "Act firm" yet "be flexible," "set high standards" yet "remember their fragile egos"—with students at this age, teachers, too, must continually reverse course to do their job well. In the middle grades, everything is always "this" and "not this" at the same time.

What students say in this book also underlines the importance of their relationships with each other:

- Their friendships are shifting rapidly and new dynamics are emerging between boys and girls.
- Their clothing styles telegraph all kinds of information about who kids are or who they want to be.
- Peer relationships are infused with high drama.
- Their pleasure derives not so much from misbehaving—actually, they still feel ambivalent about getting away with "bad stuff"—but from being able to tell their friends all about it.

We will see, through their words, that young adolescents bring their social world and their new personal preoccupations into the classroom with them. Alma, a seventh grader, talks about this:

You come to school with a big smile on your face, like, "Hi, I'm doing great today." But a lot of times I would be hidden away by my smile.

Confidences like Alma's remind us just how hard it is to be a middle schooler. Students at this age are starting to name some of their confusions but they cannot yet put words to others. Whatever they say about how they want you to teach them, and however they present themselves, something else may be going on inside. As we listen to the many student voices in this book, we start to understand how young people experience the tensions of growing up, and try to link these competing forces with classroom teaching and learning.

Listening closely to the students in our book will also prepare you to recognize the changing voices of your own students. During their time with you, these young adolescents are growing and developing in ways that will influence their academic work. As students develop new skills of communication and collaboration, as they gain a stronger sense of themselves in a group, as they learn to regulate their energies and attention, their learning—fundamentally, a social activity—will thrive.

THE PURPOSE OF THIS BOOK

Unlike many of the excellent books for middle-grades teachers, this book does not aim to tell you how to teach. Instead, we aim first and foremost to attune the teacher to the rewards of listening closely to students themselves. We understand that if you are wondering what to do in tomorrow's lesson, this book may not solve your immediate problem. But the more you learn how to listen to students—hearing the range of their worries, doubts, questions, and longings—the more effective you will be in finding your own methods to support the students you teach. You cannot expect your own students to blurt out these confidences in the course of your busy school day. Different kids, of course, might have very different things to say. We hope that, by bringing together the voices of *our* diverse middle-grades students for you to hear, our book will sensitize you to the possibilities within *your* classes.

In this book, students tell us how the practices recommended to you by other books actually feel from their point of view. That may help you sort out, from the other advice you hear, which strategies your students are ready for now and which may come later. Day to day, you will need to decide when to hold students to your expectations and when to change your tactics in order to meet their competing needs. The teachers who meet this challenge best have had plenty of practice in listening closely to what students say and understanding the layers of meaning beneath their words.

Because it rests firmly on the words of students, this book cannot address the full range of important issues that interest middle school teachers. To many of the questions we asked them, students would not—or could not—respond directly. They spoke of race, for example, but only in the context of teacher favoritism, not in terms of their own identity. They would reveal none of their own questions and concerns about sexual orientation. On some topics, the girls had much more to say than the boys did. Perhaps because the interviewer was a white woman of middle age, or perhaps because the interviews took place in small groups, our questions could not open every door to these young people's concerns. Many topics that perplex and fascinate adults—video gaming, healthy nutritional choices, how to group the middle school grades—simply did not hold their attention. They did, however, give endless thought to the matter of when to eat (not what to eat) at school. We had to laugh, but our book remains true to their voices.

HOW THIS BOOK UNFOLDS

We organized this book so as to immerse its readers in students' own experience of school, because we believe that, by understanding that experience, you will be able to better make the practical everyday decisions of teaching. Middle schoolers are declaring here, "More than what you do, it matters how you do it." In the next paragraphs, we set forth the structure we chose in order to lead our readers from students' perspectives to teachers' actions.

In chapter 1 ("Everything Is Off Balance"), kids in the middle grades describe themselves as growing up. They reveal the questions that preoccupy them: "Who are my friends?" "What are these feelings?" "What are the other kids thinking?" "What group do I belong to?" "Will I succeed?" Like it or not, kids do not leave these questions at the door of middle school. Instead, your classroom becomes one of the key places where they work out their answers.

This chapter shows how those questions get played out during the transition to middle school, as kids wonder, "How will I fit in?" "Who will teach me?" "What else is waiting for me?" It reminds teachers that your caring relationships with students—as shown by the subjects you bring up, by your interest and enthusiasm, by asking students what they already know about, and by encouraging them to think about who they are and who they might become—will play a critical role in students' social as well as academic development.

Chapter 2 ("A Teacher on Our Side") shows that kids don't just reserve those questions for themselves—startlingly, they put you under a microscope, too. Unlike elementary school children, many middle school kids no longer grant their teacher absolute authority, so teachers will need to renegotiate their relationship with students. In this chapter, students give forthright examples of what they hope that will entail.

They ask that you be both "strict" and "nice" and set a tone of steady firmness. They want you to find out where they're coming from (and to learn their language), but also to convey your own values. They hope you will look out for their emotional and physical safety. They need you to care about your subject and to make it interesting, listening to their ideas and inviting their questions. They want clear academic goals and hope you will help them meet those goals, recognizing their efforts and rewarding their accomplishments. For middle schoolers, this chapter reveals, you can be more than just the person at the front of the classroom. They want an honest, direct, and sympathetic teacher—one who will listen to them.

In chapter 3 ("Social Forces in the Classroom") kids show how their social perceptions affect their engagement and sense of safety in the middle-grades classroom. "We don't want to act too good," they say, and they tell of new tensions between boys and girls. Being different hurts, students here make clear, but the actions you take as their teacher can help establish a sense of classroom community, connection, and safety.

Kids emphasize in this chapter how much a teacher's fairness in response to social forces matters to them. They want you to include them in the conversation and to treat them with equal respect. They care that you reward their efforts, regarding their missteps as learning opportunities, not occasions for humiliating them. The chapter ends with a look at how much kids still count on their teacher to be "with it," and to keep them safe.

Chapter 4 ("Helping Us Grow into Confident Learners") shows how what happens at school—including their interactions with teachers—provides them with new information about themselves in their newly emerging identity as students. Their words reveal the ways in which the tone and substance of what you say and do, in all your dealings with students, affect both what they learn and how they learn it.

For example, students say, they want help when they are struggling, yet they also want to feel safe enough to make mistakes. They want challenging work and plenty of support in doing it well. A teacher's grading practices, their words show, can either help or hurt them. They offer many ideas of how teachers can help them do better in school. They advise teachers that, even in academic classes, it helps to talk about the personal issues that can affect their performance.

In chapter 5 ("Using Our Energy to Help Us Learn"), kids remind teachers that "sitting still" and "paying attention" do not always go together at this age. They ask for frequent breaks from focused academic work. They want lessons that allow them to learn in motion and games that will vary the tempo of their school day. Don't forget their growing bodies, students emphasize here; they see food as fuel crucial to their performance at school.

Chapter 6 ("Make Way for Parents") shows us how conflicted early adolescents are about their parents or guardians, just as they are about everything else in their lives. Your students want more from their parents, and at the same time they want less than ever before. They are hoping that you will be able to find the right balance between treating them as newly independent and keeping their parents informed and involved. Their comments help illuminate the issues you may face as you try to get parents into school, communicate with them about their child's progress, and enlist their support for homework. They also suggest how community and after-school programs can help students develop and thrive when they are neither at home nor at school.

In chapter 7 ("Our Transition to High School"), kids describe the tensions they feel as they leave middle school to confront the new social and academic demands of high school. They reveal their eighth-grade worries that high school will be huge and confusing, with a complicated schedule, an overwhelming homework load, and hazing by older students.

New ninth graders talk here about the fresh start they experience in high school, and their relief when the work builds on what they did in middle school.

But they also say that teachers have less time and patience for them as they learn how to balance academic and social demands. Students offer their suggestions for how teachers can help both before and during ninth grade, by arranging eighth-grade visits and summer bridging programs, peer mentors for ninth graders, and extra support for high school's academic challenges.

THINKING BACK

To prepare yourself to work in the midst of early adolescent drama, think back on your own experience in the middle grades. If you can remember how you felt with a sense of humor, you probably will have an easier time with your students. You will understand that their inconsistencies do not reflect a failure on your part. You may remember, too, that you paid more attention to the size of your feet than to the height of Kilimanjaro, or that you worried more about who liked you than you did about who was president in 1812.

Like a good middle school class, this book is meant to be both "serious and fun."

Remembering Yourself in the Middle Grades:
An Exercise for Teachers

What do you recall best about your own experiences in grades six, seven, and eight? Make some brief notes here about your most vivid memories.

_____

_____

_____

_____

_____

_____

_____

_____

_____

_____

_____

Which of those memories bring up positive emotions? Mark them with a plus sign.

Which bring up anxious or negative feelings? Mark them with a minus sign.

How many plus experiences do you have on your list?_____

How many minus experiences do you have on your list?_____

From your standpoint as an adult, does anything surprise you about your list? If so, make notes on that here:

_____

How do you think these experiences might shape your reactions to your middle school students?

_____

_____

_____

_____

CHAPTER 1

Everything Is Off Balance

"We're not really sure what's expected of us."

If you spend ten minutes with a room full of students between the ages of eleven and fifteen, they will reveal the hundreds of different people they can be in a matter of moments. Every teacher of kids in the middle grades knows this, and—even as they zoom wildly from the sublime to the ridiculous—the students know it, too.

Unlike their high school counterparts, young adolescents haven't yet gone underground with their experiments in who they want to be and how they want to behave. They try out the possibilities like actors improvising on a public stage, taking first one role and then another. Because they often don't bother to seal off their experiments, you might easily catch them in an ill-advised scene—smoking cigarettes, perhaps, or setting fires in the bathroom. It doesn't necessarily mean they have decided on a life of crime, though—they're still playing with lots of possible selves.

What are kids—and teachers—supposed to do with these new bodies, these explosive feelings, these expanding minds? No answer will be right for long. Your students are on an ever-changing journey of self-discovery, both exhilarating and exhausting.

WHAT'S AHEAD?

Many students in the middle grades are already experiencing some of the dramatic physical, social, emotional, and cognitive changes of early adolescence. The others can see what's coming.

> I don't want to be a teenager, but I am a teenager. It's confusing: the kids in my class are like acting like they're adults already. Having all this Victoria's Secret stuff, the lotions and the perfume, and doing what girls do in music videos. I think that we should talk about things, and learn more about ourselves. A lot of people are confused about their identities.   CARMELA

Though Carmela's bewilderment may seem intensely personal, it has everything to do with how students in the middle grades think and behave at school. Unlike in their younger years, their self-image increasingly derives from their social interactions outside the home—how they present themselves, how they imagine that others see them, how their peers interact with them, and how adults at school treat them.

> At school, you have to be this perfect student. And then at home, your family expects you to be that perfect child again. But with your friends, you do all these bad things, just to get away from everything you have to be.   ALMA

Later, as high school students, their identities will develop into a more distinct and individual style. But for now, kids find themselves changing hour by hour—and everything seems perpetually off balance. When they talk about their worries, they raise the following questions again and again.

Who really are my friends? As they start to form social connections in the middle grades, kids experience both security and danger. They need and want friendships—but they discover that their middle school friendships often come at a price. As Alma describes above, "being bad" with friends might offer a respite from the demands of adults. On the other hand, students at this age are just as likely to feel compelled or coerced by the expectations of their peers.

Kenson and Edward describe the new set of pressures that awaited them in sixth grade.

> In middle school, it's harder to focus, because we have a lot more peer pressure. It might be, "Let's jump this kid," or something. You'll do it, but it's not like you have a choice.   KENSON

> If you go to a school where people swear and do bad things, [even if] you didn't do that stuff in elementary school, it's sort of hard to stop yourself from doing it. You don't want to stand out, since you're basically the only one that doesn't do that thing.   EDWARD

Rachell and Carmela describe feeling the same kind of pressure, but from a girl's point of view.

> Back in middle school, everybody wanted to be like everybody else. If you weren't like that, you got picked on. In eighth grade, everybody was ghetto.

Everybody. And I was, I don't know . . . *me*. Really preppy. All my friends were different, and a lot of my friends didn't like each other. I was always stuck in the middle.   RACHELL

In sixth grade I started swearing, and also I'd try to become grammatically incorrect. I know it sounds stupid, but I was annoyed because I was always portrayed by my friends as perfect. I'm not perfect, and I actually tried to prove that to them. But then I realized that I can't do that. No one's perfect, but you actually have to try to be, because that's the only way that you'll grow.   CARMELA

They bring the same sense of heightened expectations that they feel in their friendships to their "friends" in the media.

Girls have to be a certain way, really skinny like those models that you see or those beautiful people on TV. I was *expected* to be that. I would try to dress nice, but it wasn't for me, you know?   ALMA

At this age, girls and boys alike are continually recalibrating who they are—and what they expect for themselves—on the basis of who their friends are and what they are doing. They do not yet know that their friends are similarly confused and torn.

What *are* these feelings? Whenever it occurs, the onset of puberty can dominate a student's life with unpredictable mood swings and sexual stirrings. For most kids, their new desires cause a significant upheaval in the way they regard the opposite sex.

thanks

In elementary school you're really immature. You fool around and you think that girls have cooties and stuff. In middle school, it changes; guys start liking girls and girls start liking guys. CANEK

In elementary, most of my guy friends were like my little brothers. I would push them around, we would just have fun, and you didn't think about anything. But then in middle school, you start feeling different. You're like, "Oh, I kind of like that guy." ALMA

In sixth grade, oh my gosh: I was happy and then sad, then I almost got into a fight with a boy. I don't want to talk about it, but it was funny. While you're doing homework you'll think of a guy, and you'll think about what you accidentally did, and you'll go "Man!" You'll just keep nagging yourself. CARMELA

As you get older, if you're a boy you usually separate from the girls, unless you're boyfriend and girlfriend. You start hanging with the boys. If you're supposed to talk to a girl, the girl's always, like, "Get away from me." I still hang with the girls, but not as much as before. JASON

Some middle school students experience real confusion as they look for clues to their sexual orientation. Even though most of these students cannot yet talk about their feelings, their confusion may cause tension in their friendships.

What do they think about me? Because they are filled with uncertainty about who they are and who they should act like, early adolescents are acutely sensitive to how other people—especially people their own age—respond to the self-images that they continually borrow and discard.

People do stuff to act cool. If they like girls, steal stuff, smoke and drink and things like that, they can go around bragging about it. They know it's bad for them; they just do it to show off in front of people.   EDWARD

Some kids act really tough at school for an image around their friends, because they want to be cool. When I was talking to this kid when he was with his friends, he wouldn't stop swearing, because he's trying to get in with the group. But over the phone, he wasn't swearing, he was talking fine.   JAVIER

As young adolescents become newly attuned to the social demands they face in the classroom and on the playground, they (like their teachers) aren't quite sure who the "real kid" is.

Students go into the classroom with a mask on. They act how they're supposed to be with the teacher around, but they take off that mask when they leave the classroom. In the playground, or outside of school, peer pressure is making them swear or do bad things to make people accept them.   DANIEL

To manage their anxieties about having friends and fitting in, kids often choose what appears to be the safest path, doing and wearing what "everybody else" does.

It's ironic. People want to express themselves, but when it's a free-dress day, most of us are wearing the same things, what's in the trends. Every store sells tight jeans, so it's hard for the girls not to wear tight jeans, or a shirt that's tight, or a tank top; everyone has them. And a puffy jacket with a fur trimming on the hood. If you're not wearing the right brands, then you'll get bullied. Girls and boys.   CARMELA

Sometimes the safest path also changes from hour to hour.

My friend and I liked both rock and hip hop, and we used to talk about all that. Then when she was with her friends that mostly liked hip hop, she would try to act like she didn't know what I was talking about, to be all cool around her friends.   GENESIS

Genesis felt confused and hurt when she saw her seventh-grade friend shifting from one group to another. But actually, trying on these different roles now in a social context will, by the end of middle school, allow kids to frame the questions that help them build an identity. Carmela, for example, is just reaching that point here:

It matters to a lot of people what you wear and how you act, what music you like, what race you are. I was thinking, why *do* I like to dress nice? Is it because I'm insecure, because I want other people to like me? In middle school you find out how insecure you really are and how fake you are being, doing something to please someone else.   CARMELA

What group do I belong to? As students like Genesis and Carmela show us, young adolescents observe the groups that are forming and re-forming around them with great interest. They see that a group gets its definition by what the kids in it like to do, wear, and talk about. So they gravitate to the temporary mooring of a group that might help them answer the questions, "Who am I?" and "Who are my friends?"

Most of the time, it's just girls or just boys [who hang out together]—
unless some are brave enough to break the group. One group of girls
always brings a jump rope, and so some boys will get in that group and be
jumping rope, trying to get in. Most of the groups have a major thing they
like to talk about. There's one group that likes to go to the library. Boys that
like football a lot. Others that like to hang out and beat up on kids. There's
girls that just like to hang out and talk.   JASON

There's a girl popular group and a boy popular group, and a Spanish girl
popular group and a Spanish boy popular group. Then there's the normal
people and the geeks, and the people who don't stay with anything, people
who skateboard. And the groups of people who are really athletic—mostly
the popular boys—and the girls who act like they're hanging out with them.
GENESIS

But the group can unbalance an early adolescent, as well. It acts as a light-
ning-fast gossip mill, spreading rumors about alliances or enmities they may
not even intend.

If you even just hang out for, like, a few minutes with an opposite gender,
then they already think you like that person. At lunch I sat down next to [a
boy]. We started talking, 'cause he skateboards and so does my brother. So
we just talked about whatever, and then I stopped talking, just minding my
business. Then a whole bunch of girls come up to me: "Oh, do you like him?"
And I'm like, "No, what are you talking about?" Then they go to him: "Oh, do
you like her?" And he's like, "No I don't like her." Then it ends up being
gossip of "this person likes that person." It just happens like that.   GENESIS

> It's a thing that builds up and then drops. If someone [from your group] finds out you like someone, and then it turns out to be gossip, it'll stay there for a day or two, or a week.   JASON

Group boundaries are somewhat permeable in middle school, but not completely so. Middle schoolers are newly aware of the way that their identity is shaped by their membership in such groups, which might be defined by musical tastes, clothes, sports, computer games, or even just the manner in which they navigate the corridors.

> When I came, the kids from my old school, we'd always be hanging out in a group. Then some other kids they just hang by themselves, they be coming in the group 'cause they don't know nobody. We're just the group that likes to walk around and stuff. We only knew like three girls in the beginning of the year, all of us. Now we probably know every girl that goes there.   JASON

Kids also recognize how they are sorting themselves into racial and ethnic groups. Here it grows more complicated. Some kids might regard these groups, too, as permeable—alliances that they might try to join or to avoid, simply because they want to. Twelve-year-old Kenson, who is African American, reveals a growing awareness that race and ethnicity create barriers that are not easy to cross:

> There are three white kids in my school and one's this kid who people always pick on, I guess because of his color. He tries to be friends with people, and every year, he always gets beat up. This year, he started trying to swear and be tough, and he just got more beat up.   KENSON

Many kids at this age begin to realize that people do appraise them based on the groups they belong to. They themselves, in fact, might cling dramatically to such group identifications. They will claim their music or their hanging-out associations, as well as the racial or ethnic groups they belong to. But as they grow up, they recognize and dislike it when others reduce them to a stereotype. Just as many adults do, they quickly turn scornful and resentful when a teacher—or anyone who is not in the group—makes a characterization based on them being "skaters" or "brains."

Race, ethnicity, and family backgrounds are all characteristics that kids have not chosen, however, and they come loaded with meanings. Students are newly aware of the unspoken ways in which color and class matter, in the classroom and on the playground.

> At my school, there are mostly African American or Spanish kids. Most people try to act "ghetto," they think that's cool and everything, but it just really isn't. When a white kid starts swearing and stuff, people look at them and say, "What are you trying to be like?" When an African American kid does it, they just say "Oh, that's normal for him." I think that's ignorant.
> JAVIER

> In my school, people expect the black kids to be rude. Most white kids, if they start acting rude, people will look at them with shock. But if a black kid starts acting rude, it's like, "Oh, you're from the ghetto." Like, "Probably they were raised that way." You should think about it before you start judging someone, because not all kids were raised the way you expected.
> AMELIA

Often, students like Javier and Amelia have no place where they can talk about the complicated mix of assumptions and stereotypes they are navigating. They are beginning to critically question racial identification, and they need safe places in which to do so.

What Do I Know About Myself?

Middle schoolers learn about themselves by locating themselves in their social world. The following statements by students reveal a developmental progression.

At first, they compare themselves to their schoolmates in appearance, stature, color, and other physical characteristics.

> I'm taller than most people in my grade, and some people in the next grade.   EDWARD

> Everybody thinks I'm so little, but my friends they all look up to me. When they call me "shorty," I'm like, "Hey, that's how I'm made, I can't help it." I have a lot of mouth, but I can back it up. I do the right thing. People do pick on me, 'cause I guess my voice is deep and squeaky. At least some people like it. I wear glasses, but that's okay, 'cause I'm pretty no matter what. I'm not conceited but I know my mom did not make no ugly kids.   THEA

> My weight, maybe, is more than what it's supposed to be for my grade. And my personality, it's more loose, more "mess around." Not uptight. Fun.   GABE

> I stutter. It's not a big deal, I still talk, but most kids don't stutter and some kids stutter worse than me, so it don't matter.   ERIC Q.

Next, they start making distinctions based on what they do.

In class when people aren't doing their work, I do my work and I'm not talking. I don't hang with that many people, so I don't get in much trouble. I can't read that good, there's some words I can't pronounce, and this lady she'll come in and help. Other kids, they'll get those big words, but I'm the person who don't.   KATELIN

Some people talk about videos on TV or whatever, and I don't really pay attention to that stuff. Sometimes I act like I know about that stuff, but I really don't.   ERIC F.

I'm one of the youngest eighth graders, 'cause I'm twelve years old in the eighth grade. I act different than everybody else—individual. I don't like to follow people. Sometimes that makes it harder for me, but some people like the way I act.   AMANDA N.

I'm the one that cracks a joke and makes everybody look on the bright side and be not mad anymore. In gym class, the kids call me a geek. They don't pick me on the football team a lot. But I won a couple of games for my team, so now they know that I've got the brains and the athletics.   DENUE

They will eventually weave together images of their social selves, as they create the stories of who they want to be. They are laying the foundation of an adolescent identity.

I'm not shy. I'm not scared to go up out of nowhere on the bus and start singing to my favorite song. I have a lot of things that I'm

(continued)

insecure about but I try not to show them, 'cause when you do show them, that's what bullies pick on.   ALMA

People know me as smart and good at football and most of the time in basketball. Kids would say that I'm like a geek. I like doing my work, and I always listen to the teacher. But then, as the year went on, people would just look past that and be my friend. They decided to notice me for who I really am. I'm comfortable now.   KENSON

I try to be different. I don't sway with the wind, like what that poet said on the commercial for the anti-drugs. I love that poet.   CARMELA

I want to adopt Carmela

WORRIES ABOUT SUCCEEDING

As they deal with these social and emotional pressures and learn the new systems of middle school, many of your students will feel that staying organized and focused on academics is an impossible task.

My middle school has twelve hundred kids, so you don't really get to know the teachers that well. You have six different teachers and a lot of homework, you're worrying about your grades, and sometimes it's just kind of overwhelming.   ANASTASIA

Having more teachers makes it harder to keep track of the homework, 'cause you have to remember to give it to a certain teacher.   CANEK

Some students receive letter grades for the first time when they get to middle school, which can result in their feeling either pressure or pride.

In elementary school you don't really think about your grades. In kindergarten through second grade, the teachers just checked a box if you demonstrated a skill or you still needed that skill.   DANIEL

I found my true potential in sixth and seventh grade. I can really get straight A's on my report card, and it feels good to know that you can do something really good. You find out how good you are, and then you try your best. You don't want to fail, because you're just throwing your talents away.   CARMELA

An increasing emphasis on the results of eighth-grade standardized tests, tough policies holding back eighth graders who do poorly, and a concern about college admission that reaches down even to the middle grades have all given new middle schoolers the sense that the stakes are high.

You really have to pay attention in middle school. Don't just play around, so in high school you make a good first impression. Everyone tells me that your freshman year is your most important. Instead of your senior year, colleges look at your ninth grade year and your test scores, and see if you succeeded, or if your test scores go lower.   ASHLEY

As Ashley reminds us, students at this age really want to flex their academic muscles and to feel competent and effective in the classroom. At the same time, they feel an equally strong pull to develop social connections in their peer group. The secret of a great middle school classroom is allowing them to fulfill both of these pressing developmental needs.

SCHOOL IS OUR PLACE TO PRACTICE

In your classroom, you can help create a community that both develops your students' capacity to succeed at challenging academic tasks and help them grow into socially competent young adults. You will be making a place where they can practice becoming themselves. That means that you will sometimes be driven crazy by what seems like an endless back-and-forth between their social and their academic development.

If you clamp down on the social impulses of your students, you are pushing against a force of nature: the momentum of early adolescent development. Yet if you passively accept them, your classroom lapses into chaos.

Students give you another option, however, as they tell you regularly and directly how they experience this period of intense growth and transition. Rather than try to suppress the changes and contradictions that your students play out every day, you can attempt to work *with* them. School then becomes their place to practice new ways, which can grow, with time and encouragement, into new attitudes and habits.

Rather than choosing between structure and spontaneity, for example, a teacher can use both structure and spontaneity to capture and focus kids' energies. The same goes for the many other opposites that middle schoolers embody:

- Kids want the familiar along with the exciting, the concrete along with the conceptual.
- They want the safety of belonging to a same-gender group, but they want to try their wings in a mixed group, too.

- They must learn to collaborate, but they still may need a quiet place to work on their own.
- They want choices, but they need you to direct them and keep them focused on learning.
- They want to like you, but they will also push back against you.
- They want you to listen to them, but they may not want to listen to each other.

From adults, they seek both comfort and challenge. You can't prevent kids at this age from bringing their social preoccupations into the classroom. As Denue observes below, they sometimes become so distracted by their social relationships that they don't pay attention to the other reasons they go to school.

> You see kids running up to other people and starting gossip, asking them, "Do you like this person, do you like that person?" When you look at it, those kids are the ones who don't pass; they stay back a couple of times. That's just always on their mind. To them, that's the most interesting part of school.   DENUE

But a middle-grades teacher can turn that reality into an asset—harnessing it in the service of academic learning, while at the same time supporting the social learning that students also need in order to make progress. As you both nurture and structure their desire to feel connected socially, you will be building the likelihood that they will express their desire for competence and effectiveness through academic achievement.

TEACHERS CAN HELP FROM THE FIRST DAY

As middle school draws near, students look forward to some of the changes it will bring, and they dread others. Each change presents them with a challenge that holds both opportunities and dangers. By learning what your students' most pressing questions are, and attempting to answer them directly, you will be respecting their efforts to identify and meet these new challenges. The students who helped write this book identified several questions they asked in their first few weeks of middle school:

How will I fit in? The grapevine tells kids that they will be leaving friends from the early grades and entering a place where they will almost certainly not know many of their classmates. They fear that everybody else will have friends, but not them.

Tiffany remembers her first weeks in sixth grade at a large middle school that drew students from many different elementary schools.

> They had all their friends, because they came from different schools. The first week, I had no friends. It was me by myself, doing my work, not talking to nobody. People used to look at me like I'm a weird person, until my [old] friend came and I started talking to her. Then I started getting to know more people.   TIFFANY

They also notice that middle school holds out a chance to redefine themselves—for better or worse—in the eyes of both teachers and peers.

> When you get in trouble in elementary school, you're afraid that something really bad is going to happen to you. But in middle school, I guess kids

don't care anymore. They're like, "So what?" One of my friends from fifth grade went from good to always getting in trouble in middle school. I guess because she's older she thinks she can do whatever she felt like doing.   GENESIS

They want the status they will enjoy as older students, and at the same time they worry about fitting into a new social and academic scene where new rules of the game will apply.

In middle school it's better, 'cause you get the older kids and not the younger kids who are annoying and immature.   ERIC Q.

In elementary school, you're mostly a baby—the teacher's always there, you got to walk in a line. But in sixth grade, it's like you're all by yourself. All my friends went to other places. My first year, I felt like I didn't belong in middle school.   KENSON

They give you leeway in sixth grade, knowing you just came out of elementary school, and not that much is expected of you. But then they start to tighten down the seventh and eighth, 'cause they getting you prepared for high school.   GEOFFERY

Who will teach me, and how? Many kids eagerly anticipate the new variety in middle school, when they will no longer have just one teacher for most of their classroom time. But they also worry about the unpredictable differences among their teachers.

In elementary school, you don't have to remember all those things [from class to class], 'cause one teacher teaches everything. In middle school you have six different classes.   DENUE

> It's like you're in middle school and in elementary. The teachers act a lot different to us—they teach the same subjects, but in different ways. KATELIN

Some aspects of having more teachers they like, and some they don't.

> It's better to go to different teachers who explain to you different stuff, instead of staying in one room and learning it all at one time. ERIC F.

> It's crazy—you get more homework and the teachers expect more from you. It's crazy. CANEK

Underneath these other worries, students really want to know whether their teachers will like them and welcome them.

> The first day when I got to fifth grade, I got to know every single teacher, [to see] if they were going to be nice to me, or harsh or mean. DIANA

What else is changing? Despite everything they have heard ahead of time, most new middle schoolers face surprises once they get there. The summer before she started sixth grade, Tiffany and her Spanish-speaking parents got a letter from her new school, a small school within one of New York City's large "intermediate schools." But they misunderstood the part informing them that she would have to wear a uniform there.

> I was, like, "What uniform to wear?" So I took a white-collar shirt and I put it on, like on top of the clothes normally people wear, jeans and everything. The principal was, like: "You can't wear that. By tomorrow, you have got to wear blue, khaki, black, and a black belt." I just looked at him—because I had already got my nice clothes and my shoes! My mom had to rush that

same day and go buy my uniform and take it back home, then nothing fit me, and I had to go back to the store. It was a mess.   TIFFANY

Gabe was startled to find that middle school didn't give him time to run around or relax:

In middle school you don't have breaks. The only breaks you have is passing period. But it's not really a break cause you have to hurry up and get to your class. I think that they should have recess like in elementary school.   GABE

Once she got to seventh grade, Chanté also discovered that her teacher had a new attitude toward academic work. Though her school kept students with one teacher through eighth grade, they scheduled fewer breaks for physical activity in the upper grades.

It makes it harder, 'cause we're all stuck in one classroom. Basically, all we do is work, and once we're done with one subject we move on to the next subject. We might get a break for one or two minutes, but we don't get a chance to get up and do whatever we want.   CHANTÉ

TEACHERS CAN HELP IN THE MOVE UP

As well as helping your students "play well with others," you have an important part in helping them explore new aspects of themselves. By the subjects you bring up for class discussion or the opportunities for service you organize, for example, you convey that kids can make a difference in other people's lives.

My school's not like most schools, where most kids don't really participate, or some kids are more into it than others. At my school everyone's real into

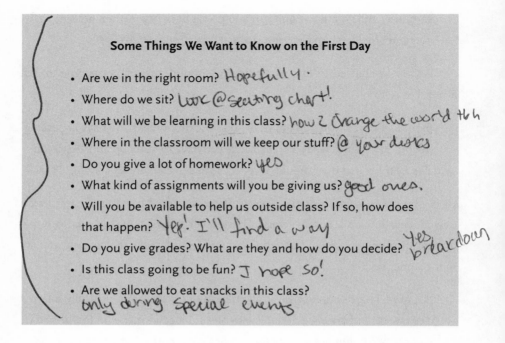

Some Things We Want to Know on the First Day

- Are we in the right room? *Hopefully.*
- Where do we sit? *Look @ seating chart!*
- What will we be learning in this class? *how 2 Change the world th h*
- Where in the classroom will we keep our stuff? *@ your desks*
- Do you give a lot of homework? *yes*
- What kind of assignments will you be giving us? *good ones.*
- Will you be available to help us outside class? If so, how does that happen? *Yes! I'll find a way*
- Do you give grades? What are they and how do you decide? *yes breakdown*
- Is this class going to be fun? *I hope so!*
- Are we allowed to eat snacks in this class? *only during special events*

it. It's all cooperative. You can be comfortable and share what you want to say, so boys and girls both talk a lot. We focus on a lot of the political stuff and how we can change the world or the country.   CANEK

When we get into eighth grade, we can help seventh graders with math or English or science or social studies. When you are in seventh you get to help the sixth graders. When you're in sixth grade, you get to help the fifth graders. I think it's important.   DIANA

By showing genuine interest and enthusiasm for a subject, teachers can inspire kids to explore new areas of knowledge—and thus new ways to see themselves. Denue's sixth-grade teacher noticed that they shared a passion for geography.

> Since I was in fifth grade I started taking notes on countries and their capitals. So my teacher would stay after school and spend half an hour going over maps with me. We started with the U.S. and then we moved to South America, and that's where I left off. Someday I want to visit all the countries and their capitals and learn more about them.   DENUE

By asking students what they already know a lot about, noticing what they respond to, and asking what they wish they knew more about, teachers invite learning on several levels. At first, kids' ideas may seem unrealistic or irrelevant to academic subjects. But it only takes a few steps to get students reading, writing, or otherwise investigating a subject that has caught their imagination. In those moments when their own curiosity leads them, they will be learning not just about the subject, but also about themselves. And that opens doors to more learning, both about the world and about themselves.

Sometimes students have interest or prior experience in subjects that teachers would not realize if they didn't probe a little. Inquiring about how they spend their time outside of school can yield all kinds of useful information about who kids are and what they know.

For example, Alma, Gabe, and Carmela all attended a summer "bridge" program for middle school students in their city, and discovered a new interest in science:

> I learned about the microscope, about its different parts and everything. Before, I didn't know anything about biology.   ALMA

> I learned how to dissect a cow's heart.   GABE

my daughter { I learned about physics, why if a car stops, you jerk forward because of inertia.   CARMELA

Alma, Gabe, and Carmela are providing clues to what they remember about their summer, and they are inviting you to take those clues and use them. Now, an English teacher might use Gabe's memory of the heart muscle to connect to a poem about a broken heart. A science or math teacher could pick up on Alma's memory of the microscope—does she know how magnification works?

Knowing more about students' nonacademic interests can also help you understand them better. A friendly question once in a while lets a student know that you care about him or her as a whole person, not just as an entry on the grade sheet.

Soccer runs in my family—my brother, he's really good at it. Now I'm on a soccer team at school, but I haven't been playing for three years, so I'm getting back on what I missed out on. I'm not the greatest, not the worst. I just really like playing.   GENESIS

As you encourage your students to think about who they are and who they might become, they are also reaching out into a new intellectual world—one where they will make close observations, recognize patterns, analyze cause and effect, and test out new ideas. That "transferability" also goes in the other direction: your academic coaching helps them develop the habits of thought they can apply to their personal and social development.

Toward the end of middle school, after your students have practiced this during their early teenage years, you will see them begin to incorporate the very process of learning into their definition of themselves.

When We Talk About the Future, Don't Laugh

Middle schoolers are just beginning to imagine that they will have a place in the world, and their first ideas about it may be unrealistic. They still answer the question, "Who do you want to be?" by telling you what they want to do. But the images they come up with are planting seeds for a picture they are building of themselves—and they don't want people to laugh at it.

Here's how two kids responded to the question, "Can you tell me something that you really want to know and be able to do two years from now?"

> When I grow up I want to get my contract to the NBA. I'd get my contract when I'm eighteen, but I'll know when I'm sixteen. JASON

> I think that by the time I'm sixteen, I would want to skydive. I think it's actually pretty cool, jumping out of a plane. GENESIS

School is something that's getting you beyond in your life. I don't want to stay in the streets like mostly people do who should know better. If you don't pass and you get a bad grade, you're never going to get nowhere in life. TIFFANY

↳ wish the focus were more "if you don't care"

In middle school, teachers always give you these projects: "Who are you?" Before I was like, "Why do I have to write about myself? That's boring."

But now I'm like, "Who am I, really?" I realize now how important that is to me. CARMELA *that's my girl!*

For kids to get to that point, however, they will need a sturdy set of supports along the way. In the next chapter, students talk about how teachers can provide those supports, through the strong relationships you establish with them in the classroom.

SUMMARY
Everything Is Off Balance

- We're wondering what to expect from you—so ask us what our questions are.
- We build our sense of self by watching you and each other.
- We need room to try on different images of ourselves.
- We might try on different friends, too, as we try to fit into middle school.
- We want you to show a real interest in who we are and what we care about.

CHAPTER 2

A Teacher on Our Side

"An ideal teacher understands and pays attention to the kid.
They should be friendly, but not too friendly."

S tudents in the middle grades bring into the classroom a muddle of expectations about what they want and need from the teacher. You will hear
this as they talk, in shifting ways, about issues like strictness, fairness, and
trust. But beneath all their opinions lies one longing: they want you to be on
their side.

KIDS ARE WATCHING

From their new perspective as adolescents, students in the middle grades begin
to watch their teachers in new ways. They notice every little thing about who you
are, what you do, and how you do it. They are always assessing what they see: Do
they trust you, or not? Do they want to be like you, or not? Do you respect them,
or not? Are you on their side—or not?

As a teacher you will feel that scrutiny—and often, it can hurt. In elementary school, kids tend to like their teachers. In middle school, they don't hesitate to remark audibly on every detail about you—how you talk, what you wear, even your personal grooming.

> My teacher's nickname was Hairy, 'cause her arms was hairy and she had a lot of hair on her body. I gave her that nickname. So she got mad at me and suspended me.   KATELIN

> The math teacher, when he's talking, people be like, "He talks like the Queer Eye guy" on TV. So when he's explaining, nobody listens, and they start making fun of him. Like he goes, "X times this equals this," and they go, "Wooow."   AMELIA

> My science teacher has an accent and people crack on him because of the way he talks.   KENSON

> My pre-algebra teacher, people made fun of him. He's got a funny accent 'cause he's from South Africa. And he got google eyes, too. When he's looking at someone, the eyes go up, like he's looking at someone else, so it's all weird. People say stuff about him, and he can hear everything 'cause they're so loud. They've got big mouths.   JASON

Kids don't necessarily intend such comments to sting. Their surveillance is just another part of their finding their own place, and defining yours, in a social world. It might help to expect remarks like this beforehand, summoning the self-confidence and sense of humor to roll with them. Eventually, you will develop an ear for when kids' comments (about you or about each other) cross the line from candid appraisal into malice—and you will also find ways to help them learn the difference. *you don't want to give us ways?*

BEYOND "BECAUSE I SAY SO"

Just a year or two ago, your students saw their teacher as the central figure in their lives at school. They regarded the authority in the classroom as coming from behind the teacher's desk. But starting in the middle grades, authority stops being so simple.

For one thing, by the end of the middle school years, many of the students will be as tall as their teachers, or taller. This alone causes them to reconsider the basic premise of adult authority.

> When we were little, we were, like, "I'm going to behave because that teacher is bigger than me." But now that we're almost the height of those teachers, we're just too comfortable with the teacher. So we say to each other, "Whatever, we're going to misbehave because she's almost my height and oh, she's cool with me." Some teachers get mad, saying, "You'd better not say that, because I'm not one of your friends." DIANA

For Diana and her friends, their new stature challenges the unspoken simplicity of teacher-student relationships in elementary school. They now see themselves as similar to their teachers, yet different. They spend a lot of time and energy exploring the boundaries of these new relationships.

Early adolescents no longer see themselves as a block of kids in a classroom with you at its head, but as part of many shifting group alliances—which may include the teacher, or not. To make things even more complicated, they also now have several teachers in the middle-grades classrooms where they are seeking their roles.

From this perspective on the bridge between elementary and high school, your students continually renegotiate your authority. How they respond to you keeps changing. They might react to you based on how you look and speak, then shift to whether they think you like them. Their response may come from how they perceive the way you treat them, or how you react to their learning needs. It may depend on how they are feeling about themselves and their peers.

> A lot of kids don't have anybody to look up to. Somebody that you know— to follow in their footsteps, to learn from their mistakes, or just to help out—it's really hard without that. Teachers can be like that, but a lot of teachers aren't. They teach you social studies, and just that. They don't find that special bond or connection with you. You're not looking forward to going into their class, 'cause you know it's not like your friend that's teaching. It's not a comfortable environment, it's a person that you have to follow strict rules by. You don't feel comfortable saying, "I'm starting to go through changes, I need help. I'm not sure what to do, I can't talk to my family." Kids don't feel secure about themselves. They're not confident, so they do all these other things.   ALMA

As Alma observes, kids are still working out what kind of relationship they can have with a teacher. Still, your role does loom large in their eyes—and it is not all about academics. Much more, they are watching closely for signs of whether you are on their side.

They will find that evidence in different forms, depending on their age and outlook. At first, kids may just see it when you are willing to be playful with them and smile, when you let them get away with some things (but not too many), and when you offer the tangible rewards they understood as younger children. Later, they will see that you're on their side when you want them to do well and succeed in school.

Either way, the evidence will come from your respect and caring for students, your trust and confidence in them. Kaitlyn, for example, saw those qualities in her eighth-grade math teacher:

> She was real down to earth, really talkative, but she was also very . . .
> "teachative"—I don't know what word. She was very smart. She'd teach
> you. She'd try with you until you got it, and she was real nice. She'd offer to
> stay after school, so you could go there if you didn't get it.   KAITLYN

Students are also quick to notice when that evidence is missing in your daily interactions.

> In middle school, it's more of a big group, so they don't really focus on you.
> They need to keep you under control to teach what they have to, and so they
> don't really have time to talk to you. We're not talked to about feelings, or
> stealing, things like that. But I think it's more important to talk than to learn
> *everything*.   ANASTASIA

Even though they want to see their teacher as a person, kids also need to be able to count on you as an adult role model. They look to you for the security, consistency, firmness, and balance that seem so hard to find in their own ever-changing lives. They want you to be comfortable with them, but to act like an adult.

An ideal teacher understands and pays attention to the kid. They should be friendly, but not too friendly or else they'll lose their authority. But they have to be comfortable with the kids, and be fair to everybody.   CANEK

If you're too nice with the kids, we'll start treating you like a kid and not give you any respect. We'll think we can get away with stuff, like talking back.   EDWARD

Sometimes during class, our teacher would tell us a little joke, and we used to laugh. Then she would say, "Let's get back to the lesson, but if there's some people that can't handle a joke and finish [laughing] when I tell you, that means we're going to end the joking and the stories."   DIANA

"It's not just what you do," these kids are saying, "it's how you do it." The middle school teacher is always going back and forth between being "on their side" in the moment and helping students move beyond who they are right now.

When you strike the right balance, kids see that you regard their minds as interesting, that you trust them to take on real responsibility, and that they are people important enough for you to spend your time on. They start to believe that you will support them in the activities of learning. They feel understood and liked. They see themselves as part of the process of making and enforcing rules. Some are beginning to understand that you regard them as individuals, each with strengths and with areas they need to develop.

SHOWING YOU'RE ON KIDS' SIDE

Establishing these habits of respect begins in the very first days of class, as your students look for signals that reveal your attitudes and beliefs about them. Asking them about themselves at the start will show that you want to know them better, and it might also reveal what expectations or worries they bring to your class. (See the questionnaire on pages 47–49.)

When you help students break the ice and learn each other's names, when you establish some processes and ground rules, when they understand what work your course will include, they will pick up your signals.

If you make these details clear but not too overwhelming, kids feel secure in their role as learners. You can reassure students with a concrete sense of what you expect at the same time that you convey your positive attitude about them.

You signal that you are on the side of your students when you ask them to help create class norms for working together on academic tasks. Soon, those habits may start to carry over into their social interactions outside class. For example, your class might decide together on routines to follow when conflicts come up, whatever the problem may be.

> We have a town meeting and the seventh graders come with the eighth graders. Or we get a partner with the seventh graders, and then we talk about our thing and tell them how we feel and stuff like that.   THEA

You can teach students such positive interpersonal routines, even before they are quite ready to adopt them. In seventh grade, Katelin still expresses a concrete, reciprocal perspective on "respect."

> If an eighth grader is disrespectful to me, I'm going to disrespect them back. Sometimes they take forever in the hallways, so you have to give them a push. KATELIN

Like Katelin, many middle school students are not yet ready to make your classroom norms part of their personal codes. For that reason, it's not enough to "work out" classroom norms with your students. You will also need to refer back to those norms throughout the school year, especially when breaches (like a shove in the hallway) occur.

Kids are outgrowing their elementary school routines, but they aren't quite ready to take charge of their own routines, as high school students will. What they want from their teachers reflects this in-between status, as we see in their comments below.

Be strict and be nice. Middle schoolers want their teachers to act both strict and caring—and how to walk that line can perplex the best of us. When does playful turn into out-of-hand? When does strict turn into unfair or harsh? To make it harder, the line is not the same for every kid, or on every day. At twelve, Edward sees what his teachers go through:

> If teachers are too strict and stuff, kids make fun of them; they talk behind the teacher's back. Some people hate the teachers so much they start writing bad things about them on the walls, like "she's mean, she's ugly." But then if you be too nice to the kids they're not going to take you so serious. So it's hard. EDWARD

As difficult as it is, walking that line is one way you show that you are on your students' side when it comes to helping them learn. Tiffany, a seventh grader, imagines herself as a teacher meeting her new class:

Who Are You?
A Questionnaire for Students

filled out as me in MS

Note: I will not share your answers with anyone without your permission.

Basic information:

Name: _____

Name you like to be called: _____

What is your date of birth? _____

Your email address: _____

Your home phone: _____ Your cell phone (if any) _____

Parents' or guardians' names: _____

Do you have brothers or sisters? If so, what are their names and how old are they?

_____

Which ones live with you? _____

Others who live in your household? _____

_____

Where were you born? _____

What language do you speak at home? _____

Are you new to this school? Where were you before? _____

_____

How do you get to school? _____ How long does it take?_____

About your activities and interests:

What do you do after school? _____

_____

What would you like to do after school? _____

_____

What are some other things you really enjoy doing? _____

_____

What time do you usually go to sleep? _____

What time do you usually get up for school? _____

About the way you learn:

Do you like this subject? Why or why not? _____

_____

_____

What would you really like to learn about in this class? _____

_____

_____

How much homework do you expect? _____

_____

Describe the way you learn things best. _____

_____

_____

_____

How do you feel about working in groups? _____

_____

_____

Is there anything that makes this class especially hard for you?

_____

_____

Can you think of a way I could help you with this? _____

_____

Who would you like me to tell when you do something especially well? _____

_____

Is there anything else about you that you would like me to know?

_____

_____

_____

_____

The first day, I'll not give them work. I would sit down with the students and introduce myself. To know a little about my students, I'll let them introduce themselves—play a little game, name cards or index cards, to let me learn their names, where they were born, what's their favorite stuff to do. Because if you start a lesson, like, "I don't want to know anything about you," kids are going to say, "This teacher is going to be so boring, and nothing is going to work out." But if you do something fun, it's going to be okay.

The next day, I will give them materials and expectations. But I'll just give them five or six expectations: What can they expect from me during the year, what I am expecting from them. What are they going to learn during the year. What is going to be the situation.   TIFFANY

Tiffany recognizes that it works well when her teachers start out "nice" and lay the groundwork before they get to the hard stuff. But kids also want you to make clear your expectations for their behavior. They accept that, in order to get them to learn, you will need to vary your behavior from strict to nice.

When we first start, they say, "I have a good side and I have a bad side. I could be the nicest teacher you ever have if you show me respect. I could be the meanest teacher if you disrespect me, don't do your homework." That's what makes us think.   DIANA

Middle school students also like to make bargains. If you ask your class what helps them want to work hard, they are quite willing to spell out the details of what they consider a fair trade:

We will do more things in class if you give us less homework. Or if you give us less textbook stuff and more activities in class, we will do more homework at home.   CARMELA

If you give us time to do our homework in class, we'll turn it in.   GABE

If we all do our homework that week, let us have thirty minutes of free time on Friday.   ALMA

Even more than in high school or elementary school, students in middle school enjoy these behavioral bargains that contain an element of fun along with an element of responsibility. Their suggestions can serve as a starting point for a conversation. They also give you valuable information about the issues your students are struggling with and the rewards that will motivate them.

Students want you to help them learn while at the same time showing that you like and respect them.

It's better to be in a class with a strict teacher. You will learn more. You will respect the person. There will be no misbehaving. But she can smile every once in a while. She can tell you a joke. You can laugh. But that doesn't mean you can cross the line. When she says "Stop," it's stop.   TIFFANY

Diana goes to a largely Hispanic middle school, where speaking English is required. Her teacher struck just the right balance when he bent that rule a little for his class.

I have this teacher, he's strict. The first day, he didn't even wait: "You have to learn this, here's your homework." He told us from the start that we could call him "Mr. H" or "Big H," but when we get to know him way better, in January, we can call him "Hache Grande," which means "Big H" in Spanish. So we were confident. It's a privilege when we can use another language in the school!   DIANA

Going into fifth grade, Edward thought his teacher looked like "the meanest lady in the world."

> But when I was in her class, she was really nice. She just had a strict face. She made us do our work, but she explained it real clearly so we knew what to do, so it wasn't as hard. She also let us do garden stuff, when we finished. I tried to do everything as fast as I could, to do the gardening stuff. EDWARD

Find out where we are coming from. By showing your respect for and interest in their individual situations, you send middle schoolers the message that they matter to you. Amelia, a recent immigrant from Liberia, wished her teacher would acknowledge that students' backgrounds affect their classroom experience.

> Some of the teachers take good time to get to know you and where you came from. But some, they're just there to do what they're paid for, like: "I don't care about your country, I don't study history. I'm here to teach math, so I'll teach only math." You can show you really want to teach math. But some teachers do it with a frown on their face, and they don't let you talk. They don't really care what the kids think, and most kids end up hating them. AMELIA

When problems come up, kids notice the teachers who do not connect with them as people.

> The teachers don't really care, as long as they are getting paid. They do what they gotta do in class, and teach the kids what they gotta be taught. They don't care when students have a problem. Like, if kids say something rude, disrespectful, they just give a detention or suspension. SHANIECE

Students like Shaniece think that teachers jump right to the worst conclusions about them, and assume that you don't care about them. In the mindset of early adolescence, "If you don't care about me, I don't care about you"—so they feel invited to turn away from connection and toward resistance.

Share some things about yourself. Kids relate more readily to teachers when they can fill in some of the blanks of their lives outside school. But they don't have to—and don't want to—know everything.

> I think it's dangerous to know [about your teachers]. It's not dangerous, but you should be careful in what you talk about to us.   TIFFANY

A few human details—about your life now, or when you were younger—will bridge the gap and make learning from you easier.

> Everybody likes my history teacher, because he takes the time to talk to us in class and he makes us laugh. He makes jokes, and he talks about his kids and his new baby. He takes the time and gets to know what we want to learn, which makes him more fun, and so people pay more attention to him when he's teaching.   AMELIA

> Teachers should open themselves up and share their memories about when they were kids. My friends and I used to think that teachers were just robots, they're just there to get money and teach you a subject, but not really to help. But if you show us you have a heart, you have memories, you were a kid, then we can relate.   CARMELA

What We'd Like to Know About You

- Why did you become a teacher? Why this subject?
- Did you have other jobs before this one? What were they?
- Are you married? Do you have any kids? Do you have any pets?
- Where did you go to school when you were our age?
- What are some of your hobbies?

Set a tone of steady firmness. If you look at kids and speak to them with a firm but friendly tone, they are more likely to hear your message. They don't want to feel like anything personal is coming at them when they misbehave. They want you to treat redirecting their behavior as an ordinary matter of business.

> I love singing. But there's a lot of rude kids in chorus, screaming curse words [when we're] singing. I give the teacher a lot of respect, 'cause he don't be sitting there yelling at the kids. He'll make that person go sit down or something, but I think we deserve it if we act that bad.   AMANDA N.

> You be disrespectful to me, you give us a dirty look, you raise your voice at me, I'm gonna say something. I'm gonna be disrespectful, too. That's how I feel, I'm not gonna lie on that.   SHANIECE

Convey your own values. From how their teachers react to their behavior, kids are quick to pick up your values. That gives them another anchor when they decide how to act with others.

> My teacher pointed out how everything you do affects everyone and yourself dramatically. If I keep saying bad words it can affect other people too. If I keep doing bad stuff in front of little kids, then they'll think that it's all right. I didn't see that before.   CARMELA

Students in the middle grades want you to make clear what you think is right, model it through your own behavior, and open up discussion about it.

Learn our language. By listening to your students, both formally and informally, you let them know that you care about their perspectives. You might do this in "connections" and "reflections" circles that start and end the week, or you might get them to write to you in journal entries to which you can respond. If you don't understand the language they use, ask them about it. They may not share the answer, but they will know it matters to you.

> It helps the teacher to learn some slang. Because kids will be talking behind the teacher's back about something really bad, but the teacher won't know. There's some bad words, drug words, that kids will use, but they aren't obvious. We kind of personalize the slang.   CARMELA

In your classroom, you may have agreed on some norms that address vulgar language. But students can also learn from class discussion of the different "codes" in which they may speak—their home language, their street language, the language they use at school or in a formal setting like church. This approach also shows that you respect their different worlds and their ability to navigate across cultures.

Look out for our emotional and physical safety. The world of school can feel scary to middle schoolers trying to find their feet in the new territory of adolescence.

Very often, an adult's intervention makes the difference in how they view their chances for success.

> A person you can talk to means something. I used to have a lot of problems in sixth grade. Students start bothering you, they say they're your friend, and then they talk behind your back. One day, my mom went into school and talked to my principal, and he was, like, "I'm going to look out for her." Now I admire and respect him, because he always smiles at me and talks to me and I can trust him. Now if somebody starts gossiping and I feel bad, I tell him. He just goes to the people and says that it's going around and it better stop. Everybody listens and they stop. TIFFANY

> Sometimes we come to school really upset at something, just not in the mood, and it does affect a lot of things. Teachers do not even ask to see what's wrong; they just ignore it completely. Then they wonder, "Why are you guys not paying attention?" ALMA

> When you come from a different country, people treat you different. They don't think you know anything about this country, and they make you feel weird, kind of strange or stupid. They go, "What, can you say that again?" My teacher in sixth grade made me feel comfortable, because she allowed me to write about how it is in my country. I felt like there was actually this person interested in me, so I was unique in a way, instead of strange. AMELIA

Care about your subject and make it interesting. When you help middle schoolers experience your subject as not just important but compelling and even fun, you show that you understand what they need in order to learn.

If the teacher just gives you a bunch of work to do, and you don't like it, and the teacher seems like he don't care, you will want to pay back that teacher by acting rude or making comments. But if he asks you what you like and does it in a fun way, then you will think the teacher cares about what you like, so you want to think about what the teacher likes, and try to pay him back.   AMELIA

Finding a balance between the hard tasks of learning and the more enjoyable activities of learning can lay the foundation for your positive relationship with students.

If a teacher gives us respect, by letting us have fun, we give the same respect back. We didn't like the art teacher, because his class is boring and he gets us in trouble for no reason, so we would do things like call out loud in his class. But sometimes I would think, "What would happen if we would be nice to him?"   JESSICA

Listen to our opinions and ideas. Young adolescents need to see that their ideas can make a difference. When you give them practice in speaking their minds and put their opinions to the test in classroom activities and choices, you are building not only their self-confidence but also their critical thinking skills.

It's good to have a say in the class, to do something that we like but that helps us learn at the same time. If we gave the teacher the idea, we know we made a difference. We had an idea of something to do, and it worked to help the class.   GENESIS

My history teacher sees what we like, but he doesn't put you on the spot. He asks you something you would actually want to tell people.

If you respond, he talks back, but if you don't, he just talks to another student.   AMELIA

Invite us to ask questions. Just as important, kids need to trust that they can ask questions when they are confused. If their grasp of some concept or material is shaky, they often feel reluctant to reveal that in front of others. Your matter-of-fact and cheerful response can make them feel respected for the process of inquiry itself, not just their mastery.

My science and math teacher was just a really nice person. If you had questions, you would write a question mark on the problem and she would go over it in class.   ITAI

My phys ed teacher was cool, she understood you. She had limits; if you got out of line, then she would tell you. But you could ask her stuff and she could explain it to you, or if you needed help with something then she would talk to you.   GABE

Set clear academic goals and help us meet them. Middle schoolers feel more confident and secure when the teacher sets out achievable goals, then steers students steadily on the path toward them.

When the teacher walks through that door, she can let you know that she takes your work seriously. You need to do your homework on time, you need to pay attention in class. You will learn, and you will get to a certain point in life.   TIFFANY

Kids may hide how much it matters to them, but they appreciate your giving them the clear messages and reminders they need to meet your expectations. Many of them cannot yet hold a week's calendar in mind, and are therefore dismayed by "surprises."

> Some teachers, they just tell you on Monday that there's a test on Wednesday. You have to give kids time to study, you have to go over the stuff so we will know what to do. I stress out. I have to study all night, and I get really nervous.   EDWARD

Recognize our efforts and reward our accomplishments. It's all too easy to focus on how kids are falling short, forgetting to recognize the ways in which they succeed. Recognition matters a lot to middle schoolers, who are always trying to assess where they stand with other people. They appreciate a teacher who lets them know when they do well as a class, and they feel respected when they get rewarded for trying.

> If we respect my teacher the whole day, he'll give us extra minutes of recess, and that makes a big difference. It makes everybody in the class want to respect the teacher more.   DAQUAN

> If we behave good, he stops the class twenty minutes early and we get to go on the computer and talk to each other.   JAVIER

> If we're good and we respect her, and if we keep doing good work, sometimes my history teacher will buy us a little snack from the school.   KENSON

We've been doing testing, so he's been giving us breaks, because it's hard.   JASON

HOW FAR CAN KIDS TRUST YOU?

Much of a young adolescent's life revolves around social and emotional issues—friendships, crushes, family dramas, and other hopes and worries. These matters also affect the way a middle schooler feels about coming to school and paying attention to academics. Students suggest some ways that teachers can lay the foundation for trust.

Talking it out. In this precarious time of transition, almost any discussion—whether in the classroom, on a recess break, or in the lunchroom—offers the chance for teachers to find out what kids are really thinking and doing. As you listen to them and test their thinking with your interested questions, you are also showing them respectful ways to explore topics on which different people may take very different perspectives.

> The kids that are doing those things—getting really touchy, stealing, maybe smoking—they don't like to participate in those discussions, 'cause they think they're too cool. They're like, "Whatever, I don't need to know that." The discussions only work if the students actually feel that they can trust the teacher, that the teacher is coming from where they are coming from.   ALMA

Kids don't want teachers to act as if every risk-taking behavior is fine with them. They just want adults to treat adolescents as if they, too, can think through important choices for themselves. They don't want an iron fist to come down on them if they reveal the ways in which that process can prove difficult.

I really don't like when teachers are, like: "It's confidential, I totally understand what you're talking about." But then when you do say it— "Yeah, sometimes they try to make me smoke"—they're, like, "Don't do that!" They don't really solve the problem or help you out. They just tell you not to do it.   ALMA

Help us tell you what's happening. The trust that allows students to confide in a teacher comes only when you know them well enough to care about their personal well-being, not just their grades and good behavior. Even one adult who can establish that connection makes a huge difference to the student.

There's a teacher I had in sixth grade that really knows me, so I just feel more comfortable and secure talking to him about certain things. If I have a problem with another student or something academically is bothering me, I can go and talk to him about it. When these girls were bothering me, I went to him and he fixed it.   JAVIER

Your problems will keep on when the teacher's not there, but at least you got it out of you. You told the teacher what was happening. The teacher can handle it.   TIFFANY

As adolescents begin to explore who they are, their race, ethnicity, and gender will affect their willingness to open up with adults.

We got three black gym teachers, and the rest of our teachers is white and Hispanic. We'll go to the black people more than the others, 'cause the others wouldn't really listen to us.   SHANIECE

Kids in the middle grades seem to go back and forth between wanting adults to stand by them in their trouble and fearing that teachers will not keep their secrets. They need to know what things you will listen to sympathetically. But they also want to know what you will act on, and why.

> It's not like [teachers] are like our best friends or whatever. You don't really want to tell the guidance teachers nothing. They go and tell. They can be some real big snitches.   SHANIECE

> My friend told *me*, not the teacher, about the problem she had. And she looked like she felt released and comforted: "At last, I got this out of myself." If she tells a teacher, she thinks the teacher's going to go and tell her mother.   TIFFANY

They don't want you to tell on them or gossip with others when they confide in you.

> My biology teacher was a goofball. One day I was so mad, I was like, "I can't stand everybody. I can't wait to be a freshman." And she was like, "Oh, don't say that, 'cause once you be a freshman you're going to want to come back." It's true. I do want to come back so bad. She was a big influence. I could do my work, I could talk to her about anything. She would not tell nobody.   ASHLEY

Sometimes they do want you to intervene in a way that might solve their problem.

> One day, I had a problem in school with this girl. She kept on bothering me. But I was trying to tell an adult, a teacher, and the others end up calling me a baby. I was afraid to tell a teacher. If I had taken [care of] it myself, it would have been something way different than telling a teacher to take care of it for me. Better to talk to a teacher, even if they'll call you a baby. If you keep

on fighting about the same thing and the teacher hasn't handled it, some kids are going to be instigating a fight. I don't want to get into it. If you get in a fight, you get in trouble, get suspended, get it on your record, and it's a big mess.   DIANA

Reaching out to a teacher involves taking a significant risk, so when students do confide in you, always acknowledge their courage. Katelin, like many other students, assumes that her teachers don't really want to listen to kids' problems. In reality, teachers often simply don't know what to do about what they hear.

The teacher should take the opportunity to listen to what we got to say, if we have to talk to them sometime. Because if [it turns into] something bad, like if we hurt somebody, that's on them. They should have listened, but they didn't want to listen.   KATELIN

Teachers whose students come to them often feel as confused as their students do about what to keep private and what to bring up with other people. Most states require teachers to report suspected abuse of students, and instances in which students talk about hurting themselves or others. When you have a question about breaking a confidence, you should talk it over in general terms with a colleague you trust.

Know us, but don't expose us. A teacher often needs to walk a fine line, showing sympathy for a student without singling out the student publicly. Kids do want you to know the things that are going on with them.

The teachers might think they have you figured out, but they don't really know what happens at home. Like my aunt passed away this month.   GABE

It's hard for the student if they have family problems and then lots of homework. Teachers should know, so they can have mercy and take off some work.   CARMELA

But they also dread having personal matters brought up in front of their classmates. They may not want others to know they have confided in you, or what they have confided. So keep the information they share as part of your private interaction, and don't bring it into the class.

When my aunt died, I told my teachers, and they were extremely worried about me. They worried too much, and it kind of got annoying and bothered me.   CANEK

When they feel sorry for the person, that makes the person feel smaller than they really are. That's why people with disabilities don't like when people feel sorry for them.   ALMA

One time in school I was crying, and people were going up to me and hugging me and saying, "It's all right." And I was, like, " Just shut up, let me be alone." I don't want to make such a big deal out of it—it gets me more worked up and makes me sadder. I want to deal with it and then just keep calm.   CARMELA

As comments like these reveal, students' social relationships with peers enormously affect how they respond to you as a teacher. You may arrive in class expecting to establish a learning group in which they will take an active and engaged part. But your kids arrive with their own group dynamic already under way—and they regard it as far more compelling than yours.

In the next chapter, middle schoolers talk more about how those social dynamics with peers play out, both in and out of your classroom. The chapters that follow should help you use their perspectives toward creating a social world in which academic development can more effectively occur.

SUMMARY
A Teacher on Our Side

- Show us that you like us and find us interesting.
- Listen to our opinions and ideas.
- Hold us to the rules, but do it nicely.
- Consider our individual situations and treat us fairly, case by case.
- We want to trust you, but that's not always easy.

CHAPTER 3

Social Forces in the Classroom

"Everybody grew up together but still, we don't talk to each other as much as you would think."

The social world of young adolescents comes into the classroom with them. It can cause kids to sit with blank or glum faces while you present your most fascinating assignments. It can drive them to make inappropriate comments at moments that should elicit serious thought. Although we tend to think of middle schoolers as risk takers, they often are not taking any risks in classrooms. Instead, kids are worrying about where they stand in relation to others.

As a teacher in the middle grades, you could spend all your time trying to resist those social forces. But if you can figure out just what fears students are dealing with, you might put the currents in your classroom to good use, rather than work against them. As you help kids navigate their uncertainties, they will become more engaged, adventurous, and willing to take risks in their academic experiences. As you tune in to the issues of fairness that loom large for them, you can help them resolve some of the conflicts that keep them from learning.

WHAT'S GOING ON?

Many middle school students are aware of the competing expectations of their teachers and their peers in the classroom. They may feel pulled in different directions at different times. In the following pages, students tell us just what stands in the way of their enthusiastic response to the academic opportunities teachers set up for them.

We don't want to act *too* good. Middle school kids do recognize what a good student looks like to the teacher:

> The typical good kids stay in a line when the teacher's walking [with them]. When the teacher's out of the room, they continue doing their work. They're full of ideas, they're always raising their hand instead of just sitting there and waiting for someone to have their hand up. They do pretty good on their work, and they hand in their homework all the time.   GENESIS

But their social norms may make it hard for them to want to adopt that image as their own.

> They don't want to be embarrassed by being goody-goodies in school, and so they try to act up just to get approval from the other kids at school. Sometimes, some kids will go through physical torture, like getting in fights at school, just to fit in with the other kids. It makes no sense at all.   DAQUAN

They do care about doing well at school, and they want to be smart. But plenty of other things are going on with them, too.

One Girl's Story of Swimming the Tides

In this narrative of her social progress from second to seventh grade, Alma describes how her notion of friendship changed. Her teachers helped her, she says, even when she was pushing against them in order to have friends.

In second grade, I was a really good student. I was the teacher's pet, at the beginning. But I didn't have any friends; there was nobody that I could relate to. So I just decided to hang out with the bad students in my class, and it caught on. I was still smart, but I was the baddest little second grader you've ever seen. I would give the teachers attitude: "No! Don't boss me." Then I would be sent out of the classroom.

I started stealing when I was in fourth grade, with my friends. The same people, they were always with me. I knew what I was doing was wrong and I just kept on doing it. Nothing happened, I got away with it, then finally I got caught. I was so scared. I remember waiting in my classroom for my mom to come, shivering and crying 'cause I knew that she had trust in me and I let her down. She didn't even yell at me, she was just quiet and looked at me. I just couldn't take it and I finally realized that it does come back to you. It's like throwing away your life. I was lucky in a way to have the support of my third and fourth and fifth grade teacher and my mom and my sister. I've gotten stronger now. I've learned from that, from just seeing how much your so-called friends can hurt you. If I got in trouble, they would run away and just leave me there. The older you get, the more you start to see how big a mistake people can make, how bad people can be.

We feel new social tensions. When you ask boys and girls to work with each other in class, or help each other out, they may be uncomfortably aware that other kids will start pairing them up romantically.

> In my fourth-period class, this girl was sitting a couple of seats behind me. She was in my third-period pre-algebra class too, and she came up and started asking me did I remember what we had for homework. She sat down and I started telling her, so she could write it down. Her friends were calling her, and she was like, "Wait a minute, wait a minute." After, they started yelling things: "Oh, you like him." And she was like, "No, I don't! I'm just asking him what the homework was." And they said, "You don't have to hide it," and all this other stuff. It made me feel, like, nervous and embarrassed.   DENUE

They themselves are often confused about their motives.

> Some of my friends, they compete against each other to see who's smarter, even though it doesn't matter. But girls if they have a crush, or guys if they have a crush on the girl, they don't want to seem like they're too smart, 'cause it might seem like they're a know-it-all and ruin their reputation.   GABE

> I think it's different with girls and boys. Girls sometimes get harassed, or people make judgments about them. Because, I don't know, <u>boys just can't control their hormones or something.</u> So they make fun of girls and they start saying inappropriate stuff. Maybe it's because they like the girl. They just like picking on people. The girls might not like what they hear, but they might not want to go to anyone, because they might not feel safe.   KENSON

They are counting on you to know—even if they don't know—when they need your help. The way you react can send a clear message about what you consider sexual harassment and what is simply exploring how to interact socially.

> The girls, they're always bothering the boys, and the boys are always bothering the girls, and the teacher knows that it's just for fun. But one kid, he was bothering this girl. The teacher knew that she didn't like it, so he told the boy to stop it. JASON

Being different hurts. In the middle school years, students' appearances and capabilities vary even more widely than at other ages. Early adolescents are painfully aware of this.

> There's this girl at my school, and nobody likes her because she smells like she takes a shower once upon a Christmas. The teachers can't make you be friends with her or any other person. You choose who you want to be friends with. You wouldn't want to be caught hanging around that person, because they would think you took a shower once upon a Christmas too. DAQUAN

> I'm not saying I'm perfect or anything, but sometimes kids like to hate on people and I'm one person to hate on. I stutter. ERIC Q.

Students with limited English or students with disabilities face additional hurdles to being included as friendship groups take shape.

> There's this girl at my school, she speaks French. So people actually think she's stupid in a way. The students use her as a clown. They go, "What, can you say that again?" The teachers, I think they notice it, but they feel they can't control the kids. AMELIA

I can't read, and that's not my fault. God made me the way he wanted to make me—did I ask God to do that? I don't think people should pick on me just 'cause I can't read. They come up to me and they be like, "Read this word for me, I can't read it." I'll be like, "You know I can't read, can you get out of my face please?" They be like, "Too bad. I forgot you stupid and you in that retarded class." I be getting mad and I want to punch them and stuff. AMANDA N.

It's all too easy for students to maintain a connection to their friends by ostracizing someone who is different. Still, kids don't necessarily want to be heartless. Even when they don't speak out about someone's exclusion, they often sympathize, as we see from Javier's response to Daquan's earlier comment about a girl in his school.

I don't think it matters, just the way somebody smells or something. The way they smell doesn't mean the kind of person they are. Maybe you could just tell them, in a respectful way, "Maybe you should try showering more." Maybe you should try to be their friend. JAVIER

People think about themselves that they're too fat, too thin, too stupid, and they think that people are going to notice whatever they're insecure about. I think that it's just in their mind. People should just think positive about themselves, not think in a negative way, and that might help them a little. DANIEL

FINDING COMMON GROUND

As the year goes on, an empathetic teacher will have plenty of opportunities to help middle-grades students grow in confidence and reach out to others in pos-

itive ways. Students want to know how to find common ground without sacrific-
ing their own individuality and emerging style. School provides a context in
which they can learn about themselves and their classmates, accepting and respecting their strengths and differences.

Faced with the disparities among your students, you can offer them ways to
bridge their differences and discover what each has to offer.

> Teachers can try to find out what the kids have in common, and have them
> discuss what they have in common, so they can use that to get closer to
> each other as friends.   DAQUAN

> It's good to see how you have something in common with a lot of other
> kids. Maybe you all tell about an embarrassing moment, and then you're
> recognizing that everybody has gone through an embarrassing moment.
> Or a fear most kids might have. And afterwards, you're, "Oh, that
> happened to me once."   GENESIS

> At the beginning of this year, the teachers made all of us act silly in front of
> each other. When we're playing games, everyone is laughing at each other.
> You can see other people acting silly—not just one person. We played the
> game "Zip, Zap." One person stands in the middle and says, "Zip." The
> person he says "zip" to has to duck, and the two people shoot each other
> and say "zap." We all start laughing if we duck, or if we miss it and get in
> the middle.   JAVIER

Having broken the ice, kids will keep up the process on their own.

> This year, I met this kid and we were talking about baseball, about the
> Yankees and the Red Sox, and another kid jumped in and started saying

how the Red Sox were going to win. Then we started arguing and playing, and from that moment on, we always hanged out.   DENUE

In organizing academic work for your class, you can also encourage these connections to develop.

Instead of just having kids do individual work, do more group activities. Because in my room, there's only some people who talk to some people. There are groups. Everybody grew up together but still, we don't talk to each other as much as you would think [even though] we've known each other for years.   KENSON

There's only a small amount a teacher can do, because it's really up to the kids. But if there's a project, she could try to pair up people who really don't talk to each other, don't respect each other. They could actually learn to become friends and respect each other, knowing they're both being their selves in a way they both can relate to.   JAVIER

Matter-of-fact assignments that involve task sharing and cooperation— from a hands-on science activity to making posters for a school assembly—can help students build confidence, communication skills, and respect for each other. These skills need coaching from you, beginning with students learning each other's names and forming work groups. On their own, middle school students will otherwise make "safe" social choices of work partners, avoiding those who seem different from themselves.

Learning How to Work Together

Before plunging students into working together on an academic assignment, you may want to give them practice on a collaborative activity. In this example, students work in groups of five to reach a decision on the best way to spend an imaginary $75. (An alternative: ask them to pick what to have with them if they were stranded on a desert island for a week.)

First, with your class, develop norms for working in small groups. These might include:

- No putdowns, even in jest.
- No side conversations when anyone is talking.
- No criticizing anyone's ideas during brainstorming.
- Within each group, use "six-inch voices" (as opposed to the "six-foot voices" or the "six-yard voices" people use in larger groups).

After creating groups, have each group choose a leader, a recorder, and a reporter. (If you are doing this early in the year, make sure students know each other's names.)

Set a time period in which the groups do their work, which will culminate in their choosing the five best ways to spend $75 (or the best things to take to the island). To do this, students will first brainstorm their ideas, then work together to pick their top choices.

This is p much simplified complex instruction

Next, each group reports to the class. (Depending on the time you have, you can ask them to explain their choices, too.)

Finally, ask the students to go back into their small groups to generate answers to these questions about their process:

- What worked well in your group?
- What did your group have problems with?
- How did your group make its final choices?

During this practice exercise, you should move around the room to coach the students on listening and keeping to their norms, and to help the leaders keep their groups on task without hurting the feelings of others.

As you notice more about what's going on among your students socially, and what they care about, you will find opportunities to help them safely connect to each other in new and important ways.

Students may be afraid to say anything at all, for fear of appearing different from the others. If you structure activities for sharing different ideas, you can show them that having their own point of view is not only safe but also valued in your classroom.

As your class studies history, literature, math, and science, you will come across examples of people—Rosa Parks, Ponyboy Curtis, Einstein, Galileo—who dared to set themselves apart from a prevailing belief system. By examining such examples as social dilemmas, you can connect directly to your students' experience, asking for their thoughts on when it feels okay to speak up (in class and out) and when it does not.

KIDS CARE THAT YOU'RE FAIR

The behavior of your middle-grades students also may hinge on what they consider fair. Especially when problems arise, kids at this age often hold a different perspective about what's fair than their teacher does. Within any group, students will differ in how they think about fairness. They will all, however, express their outrage with similar vehemence when they perceive a situation as unfair.

Fairness issues often show up in the academic context. For example, if you ignore what students have to say in class, they feel dismissed.

> My teacher will get us interested in a topic and we'll all be raising our hands and wanting to say something about it. But he only picks on two people to say something, and then he goes into a different thing. I usually call out, because I'm dying to get this comment out, and then the teacher's like, "You're supposed to raise your hand." How am I supposed to raise my hand if you're not picking me at all? I feel like he doesn't really care what we have to say. He just wants to get over with the day.   GENESIS

Students look to the teacher to establish fair procedures for getting their voices heard.

> They could write names on the board and go in that order. I was in English class and I had my hand up for thirty minutes, after the teacher told me I was next. She was picking other kids, and then she looked straight at me and just picked somebody else.   JAVIER

For class discussions, we have a ball you throw to someone, and nobody talks if they don't have the ball. It keeps everybody quiet, because you don't want anybody talking when *you* have the ball.   AMELIA

But their desire for fairness in the classroom presents you with an even better opportunity. Together, you and your students can explore what they consider fair and agree on classroom rules that they can live with.

As a start, you might ask for their thoughts on what's desirable in the class-room, perhaps with questions like these:

- What does it look like when a student shows respect for another student?
- What does it look like when a teacher shows respect for a student?
- What does it look like when a student shows respect for a teacher?
- What can other people do to make it feel safe to speak up when you disagree with another student in class?
- What can other people do to make it feel safe to say when you don't know the answer?
- What can other people do to make it safe to speak up when you do know the answer?

Make us part of the conversation. Once you and your students have created a vivid picture of a safe and respectful classroom, you can take the second step of developing classroom norms of behavior on which everyone agrees. Many teachers start the year by doing this.

Having students collaborate in setting expectations for your class can be a powerful process.

We Can Work It Out

When kids get to contribute to solving a problem of classroom behavior, they are more likely to respect the decision. Here, several students talk through the issue of cell phone use.

Carmela: There's a problem in my class, a lot of people text or even call while class is starting. Watch out for people with sweaters, 'cause they hide their phones in their sleeves. I feel like a traitor saying this.

Itai: I think that teachers should ask the parents if the kids have a cell phone, and then every day the teacher can collect all the cell phones and then at the end of the day give them back.

Alma: Maybe the teachers should assign the seating order, so they can see everybody. The teacher should pay more attention and say, "Keep your hands out." Maybe they should make them take off their sweaters.

Canek: You know how they have pop-up quizzes? Maybe the teacher could have a pop-up checkup on the kid, like check the clothes that might be looking suspicious.

Itai: Teachers should call on everyone, 'cause the people that might not be raising their hands could be doing something suspicious. So then: "Can I check you to see?"

Carmela: I don't like when teachers single out people.

Gabe: If the teacher notices somebody is doing something like that, then they could just wait for a second and then bring up a subject and call on them to explain the lesson.

> The third week, our teacher decided to let the kids make up their own rules that we would follow by ourselves. It's the whole seventh-grade contract; we did it together as a community, because we didn't want the same old school rules that we had last year. Right now, it's working. We each get a contract with the rules, to make sure we're following them. We judge ourselves every day, and we are honest; if we really know that we didn't do well, we put a "no." If we do something bad, it comes back on the person who messed up. If we are following it, we put down a "yes" or a check. On Friday, at advisory [group], they check it.   JESSICA

Not all kids will be ready at once to start putting the group's needs before their individual desires. Simply creating classroom norms, as Jessica notes, does not guarantee compliance. As behavior issues come up, you will need to keep referring back to those norms. Posting them nearby makes them visible, and easy to refer to when students need reminding.

> My history teacher this year in eighth grade said some kids were eating in her class. She was like, "Okay, every time somebody breaks the rule, I'm going to refer back to the rules that's on the wall." She kept running down the list of rules, and then kids stopped.   KENSON

Middle schoolers know that they are not yet getting the moves quite right for the adult world. That's why, after they get into trouble, they'll so often promise, *"Now* you can trust me." Up to a point, it's a good idea to give them another chance. Perhaps today will be the day that they will take another step forward, embracing the expectations or norms of the classroom.

Even when kids want to cooperate in meeting the needs of the class, they may find it difficult to do so. Their attention naturally goes to other things going on around them. When the teacher is talking to the whole group, there will always be some who do not hear you—and they will probably blame this on you.

> Our teacher tells everybody but me and my friend when our class has to leave from lunch for upstairs. So we get in trouble when we get back to class, and then we have to walk upstairs every day with her. I try to say, "How come you don't tell us?" KATELIN

Students want to work with you to find solutions to these recurring problems, and they have ideas that are worth considering. When you bring these problems to them for discussion and agree to try out the things they suggest, you help them feel powerful in a constructive way. At the same time, you set the stage for future collaborative problem solving.

> When one person goes to the bathroom, then more people will want to go. After a while, when you ask the teacher, she's going to say no, 'cause she thinks that you're going to be playing around. Then it will happen to someone who really needs to go to the bathroom. They should just say, "Everyone go at once and come back." EDWARD

What Are Norms, Anyway? Curse Words as an Example

Students often aren't quite sure what a teacher means by using the word "norms" (to describe standards of behavior that the group agrees will apply to them). You can help them uncover its meaning through talking about cursing—a habit greatly influenced by the group's norms. Because cursing has a lot to do with a young adolescent's self-image, it can lead to an interesting class discussion.

For example, you might ask students:

- What is the difference between the language you use inside the classroom, the language you use outside the classroom, and the language you use at home?
- Who sets those "rules"?
- Are there words that "everybody" uses, and why?
- What groups use which kinds of language?
- What norms about language will we have in this class-room? Why?

Thinking critically with kids about the language they use also allows them to tackle something they are already working hard on—their membership in groups—and to identify the implicit "rules" that they have adopted as their norms.

What's Fair from a Student's Standpoint?
An Exercise for Teachers

Students in the middle grades vary widely in their ideas about fairness and social responsibility. Some kids still see a dilemma solely from their own point of view. Others have begun to balance competing claims and perspectives. Still others have reached the point where they appeal to a social norm to decide what's fair to all.

At any point in the school year, you can gain insight into the spectrum of how students in your class think about fairness by presenting a dilemma for them to discuss, then noticing what kinds of answers students give and how they share their ideas about working out agreements.

You can use dilemmas that emerge directly from your classroom experiences when students violate a classroom norm. Ask them:

- What norm was violated?
- Why do we have that norm?
- What is a fair response (consequence) for the student(s) who violated the norm?

- Who is responsible for keeping the class norms visible and enforced?

You might also use dilemmas from your curriculum. For example, you could present a choice made by an historical or scientific figure, or by a fictional character, that resulted in a desired goal or outcome for the actor but had negative consequences for someone else. Ask students:

- What decision was made?
- Was it fair? To whom was it fair?
- Who might have thought it wasn't fair? What other decision could have been made? Would it have been more fair? To whom? Why?

For every action students suggest, make sure to ask them to explain clearly why it seems fair to them. Make clear to them that no one right answer exists, and encourage them to share their opinions, even when they disagree with others.

At the end of the discussion, ask students to help you summarize the discussion:

What things does the class agree about? _____

_____

_____

_____

What things does the class disagree about? _____

_____

_____

_____

By reflecting on such a discussion, a teacher might learn how individual students think about fairness. Answering the questions below could help you later, when other issues of fairness come up in class.

Which students took an individual point of view and had trouble thinking about fairness from multiple perspectives?

_____

_____

_____

Which students thought of fairness in terms of a tit-for-tat reciprocity of benefits and injuries?

_____

_____

_____

Which students appealed to social norms of leadership, generosity, responsibility, promises made or broken, group loyalties?

_____

_____

_____

Now think about the students as a group. Which kinds of reasons seemed to sway the class more than others?

_____

_____

_____

Treat us all with the same respect. Students are more likely to trust you to be fair if you know who individual kids are and what matters to them.

> Many times, the kids who behave good in school, teachers don't know them that much. You have to do something bad so the teachers will know your name, so the teachers will think you're somebody.   AMELIA

On the other hand, nobody likes it when the teacher singles out someone for special treatment.

> Teachers let that favored student do more, even if it's just a little thing like moving around in the room, or leaving when you want to. As much as students say, "I don't care," they know deep inside they care.   HEATHER

> The band teacher favored this really good clarinet player. It made me feel angry, like I wasn't important to the band or they don't need me, and I should just quit. Instead of bringing up one person and leaving behind sixty-one, she could have treated everyone the same.   DANIEL

At this age, students often equate "treating everyone fairly and respectfully" with "treating everyone the same." This poses a continuing dilemma for teachers: at times, you will need to treat students differently in order to show them equal concern and respect. You may want to explicitly tell students when you make such choices. Otherwise, students will assume that your different reactions arise from differences in how you feel about them, rather than from your judgments about what each student needs from you.

Itai's teacher made it clear to her class that all students mattered equally to her, even though her reactions to them might vary from time to time. When fairness did mean treating each student in the same manner, she described how she would proceed in a way that her students could understand and accept.

> She cared about everyone. She didn't stereotype; she always said that she wouldn't be biased towards anyone. When she was grading a test, she would always cover up the names and just mark what they didn't get. Because she felt that if she wasn't proud of that student that day, maybe she would give them a lower mark.   ITAI

Middle school students also have a sharp eye for how teachers respond to students on the basis of race, ethnicity, or social class.

> Teachers should treat all students the same, no matter what color they are or how they do in school. But some teachers treat black students different. At my school, they say a whole bunch of bad stuff about us. When a student goes to tell the principal, the principal believes the teacher over the student, if it's someone who doesn't do that well in school.   TATZI

As we have seen, students are quick to notice when a teacher has a favorite. If they also perceive differences in how a white teacher responds to students of color, they may conclude that he or she discriminates against kids based on race and ethnicity.

> I had this person in my honors classes, he was the only African American in our class, and he was really funny, he was a nice person to be around. But he jumped around a lot, I guess, and you could kind of tell that these two teachers hated him. When he raised his hand, they would ignore him. I would say that they were disrespecting him because of his race. I think it was a factor.   DANIEL

I think my teacher was racist of black people. The whole year she was mean to me, wasn't letting me go to the bathroom. When everybody else asked, she would give them a pass: "Be right back." But if I asked, "No! You can't go!"—how's that sound? KATELIN

Students in the middle grades are newly attuned to evidence of racism and discrimination, perhaps unintended but nevertheless real. Teachers need to listen sensitively to their accusations and respond to them seriously. By doing so, you give them opportunities to question, along with you, the underlying meanings carried by social interactions. Thea describes a situation in which several African American students saw racism in a vice principal's actions.

Today at lunch, a white boy was sitting at a table where he wasn't supposed to, 'cause we are supposed to sit with our class. And he said that black people are ignorant. We told the vice principal and he came over and said, "Just leave it alone." If it was us, he would have said what he says to everybody: "Pick up your tray and come to the office." THEA

Your first step involves listening carefully to how students perceive the attitudes of those around them about race and ethnicity. This will allow you to reflect on the biases and preconceptions that you, like any teacher, may bring into the classroom.

Listening closely will also help you understand the environment (and their perceptions about that environment) that forms the context for your students' developing racial and ethnic identities. Talking openly with them about issues of bias and privilege will help. It encourages students to participate in exposing entrenched beliefs and practices within the adult community that limit their opportunities and achievement.

Guard our right to a fair decision. Whether kids are acting within the limits or outside them, everyone is closely watching how you respond. They will draw their own conclusions as to how fair you are.

> My math teacher, it's like he's trying to please the kids that are bad. There's this girl, she doesn't do any of her work, but he lets her get out of the class at any time. He's afraid of getting cussed. But the good kids, he doesn't let them. It's like he's punishing them for being good. AMELIA

When you need to make the call about what's fair, it helps to refer back to the behavior norms the class has earlier helped to shape. If students also have had input into the consequences, when someone departs from those agreements, your decisions are less likely to seem arbitrary or unfair to them.

Kids appreciate it when teachers find humor in their breaches of good conduct, even as they correct them.

> When people swear, I've heard my gym teacher say, "Do you kiss your mother with that mouth?" People laugh, but it makes people understand how they're acting. KENSON

Many issues of fairness require balancing the rights of the individual with the rights of the group. The students who helped write this book pointed out certain key areas in which this particularly matters to them:

Punishing everybody for what one person does. Most middle school kids hate it when the whole class gets blamed for what only some of them have done—no matter how clearly you may try to justify such an approach.

They're trying to say, "The whole class has to take the punishment, because we're all in this together." Well, for me it's not fair.
GENESIS

On the other hand, they may not know exactly what's fair when a teacher doesn't know who is responsible for the unacceptable behavior.

I guess obviously then we all gonna have detention or something like that. But they should ask, or people should tell them, or something. Don't punish the whole class. If you have to, I guess you're gonna have to do what you gotta do. THEA

Cleaning up after other people. In the world of young children, people only have to clean up their own mess (or else someone else cleans it up for them). Many middle schoolers may not yet see a shared responsibility to maintain the space their group uses for learning.

If we made the mess or we didn't, my Spanish teacher makes us pick up papers before we leave his class. He makes you clean the spot that you are sitting at. So if someone threw a paper next to your desk, or if anyone threw a paper at your desk, you'll end up cleaning up. I don't think that's fair. We didn't put it there. AMELIA

I think that the teacher should make kids clean after every period. It's their mess that they made. Nobody else should be responsible for cleaning it up. If you come into that classroom and you share that seat, the teacher might think that you made the mess. DENUE

Denue and Amelia show here that they do not yet consider themselves responsible for the actions of their peers. But as you create opportunities for kids to collaborate in the classroom, they are far more likely to see the value of teamwork. (Punishing them as a group does not provide that developmental spur.) When they solve problems together, a social perspective on the group's interests will emerge and start to matter more to them. This will eventually extend to how they see themselves in the larger school community.

Coming to class on time. Tardiness also challenges teachers to help kids see themselves as members of a group in which their presence matters. Conventional consequences like detention can have some effect, but they reinforce students' perceptions that being late is a personal issue, not a group one.

> I'm not saying you have to threaten kids for them to show up on time for school. But my teacher gave me a detention because I was late three times. That showed me. I didn't want another detention. I just showed up on time every day. JAVIER

> I think they should give us more time to get to class. Sometimes kids have to use the bathroom, and they don't get out by the time they're supposed to be there. Most teachers don't take excuses. You're trying to explain to them and they're like: "I don't care. You're late for my class, you get a detention." GENESIS

Motivating students to show up on time for what's going to happen in class tends to work much better in preventing tardiness.

> Teachers should do something good at the beginning of class to make kids want to come early. My teacher does the boring stuff first, and then he gives

kids time to relax. So most kids don't really care when they come late, and when you give them detention, they don't really care either. At the beginning of [another] class, we did this game to warm us up: If you answer some question, you get a prize. So kids came, because you wouldn't want to miss the beginning of class. AMELIA

Here again, many teachers find that humor works well. Javier and Amelia describe an effective song-and-dance ritual used at their summer program whenever someone arrives late to the morning meeting.

They just stop the whole lesson and start singing: "Pop, pop, fizz, fizz, pop, pop, fizz, fizz. Check him out, check-check him out. Check him out, check-check him out." And then—say I was late—I would have to say, "My name is Javier." And then they would say, "And that's no lie, check." And I would go, "Pop, pop, fizz, fizz," and they say, "Mm-mmm, how sweet it is." It works—you don't want to show up late, because people are going to make you do that dance. Because it is a little embarrassing to shake your booty or something. It doesn't feel *really* bad, it's better than that, but it's something that you don't want to get. It's good, because the teachers get it too, if they're late. It happens a lot. JAVIER

It's like they're laughing with you, but they're laughing at you, too. Some people don't want to do it, so they just come early so they don't have to do the dance. AMELIA

Amelia and Javier's teachers have established this playful embarrassment as a norm for their summer program, so students can consciously experience a physical metaphor for the disruption they cause to the group when they show up late. While this exercise may be too risky and time-consuming for most classrooms, other activities can help students begin to recognize and identify more with the group's needs and priorities.

> We were separated into groups of sixteen, called "families." We didn't do things individually, we did it together as a family, and the families got into competition, like chair building. When we get into stuff together and we compete, even if you don't like a person, you have to cheer them on because they're in the family. If they lose, that means your family loses. AMELIA

As more students develop attitudes like this, you can eventually turn problems like tardiness into something that the whole class can discuss and work on together.

> I think [talking about the problem] is better with the whole class. It can get chaotic, but if you really want this to happen then it will work out. Because we realized how bad we've been and we found the problem, and so we really try to work to become a better class. CARMELA

Reward our efforts with things we really want. The gold stars and stickers of elementary school no longer motivate middle schoolers. Instead, they want gestures and items that fit with their new, more social sense of self.

> A better reward is giving us funner activities. Like playing games, or academic activities that are fun. CARMELA

We have this Raven Awards system, because our mascot is the raven. When you do something good, if you do well in class, if we do all our homework for a week, then each person can get these little Raven Awards cards. When you get a certain amount, the student council hosts a pizza party or a root-beer float party, and you get to go. So you want the Raven Awards.   ITAI

In addition to actual activities, students also feel rewarded by signals that the teacher regards them with increased respect.

I don't think we should get candy. Candy kind of makes the situation worse, 'cause you end up getting hyper. [A good reward is] that the teacher will ease up on you, give you more chances, or respect you more.   GABE

Giving kids a choice can seem like a reward, as students feel they are earning your respect.

They should take a survey first, to see what would be a good reward if we finished all our work on time. Maybe some people don't want to do something that other people do, so teachers could switch off, and change it after a certain time. I really like reading, so sometimes I wish we could take a break from school and we would have time at school where we could just read. Or if you didn't like reading, you could do something else.   ITAI

Help us learn as you correct our behavior. Kids don't want to change their behavior when your reaction humiliates them in front of others. If they feel your disappointment too keenly, they are likely to withdraw or retaliate.

My science/math teacher always embarrasses kids. If you forgot your math book, or if your homework is overdue for this amount of time, she'll announce it to the whole class, instead of just telling you privately. I don't think they should do that. It makes me feel embarrassed. I just want to go away and crawl into a hole or something.   GABE

Students at this age may be newly aware that their moods affect them, but they do not yet know how to tell you directly when they are in trouble, or when for some reason they can't do something that you ask. Instead, they are hoping you will notice their situation rather than unwittingly provoke a cycle of frustration or rage.

> Teachers should know when somebody's having a bad day. They sit there and yell at us, and we're going to flip out on them. [One teacher] kept telling me to do this, do that, 'cause I was behind in work. I was trying to do my work as fast as I can, but I don't write that fast. So I kept going "Whooo! Hufff!" and sucking my teeth and stuff, just to get on her nerves. She was sitting there saying, "Amanda, be quiet, Amanda, stop." I got mad, and I just got up and left. [It would have helped me if she could] have talked to me about it—or just let me sit there for a little bit, in the classroom, and be me.   AMANDA N.

If other kids are watching, a student might directly challenge your authority ("Why you in my face?"). You can answer the challenge quietly, drawing the student aside to say that you are there because you care. When you let students save face by addressing their issues in private conversation, they are much more likely to shift toward a more positive action.

The way in which you impose consequences can make the difference in whether kids learn from their mistakes. They need both your insight and your firmness.

> A lot of times teachers are, like, "Don't make these mistakes." But the reason why I am how I am right now is because I learned from my own mistakes. We're going to learn from the consequences, whether it's a time

out for a five-year-old or suspension for a thirteen-year-old. I think it's necessary for kids, especially our age—not too much, but a little bit, so we know not to do them.   ALMA

When you decide to call home about a problem with their behavior, kids still want you to be on their side. Let them know that you will be calling, and why. You might also want to find out what fears they may have about your calling home. If you are clear about your goals in making the call, the long-term outcomes are likely to improve.

I've noticed that the only reason teachers ever call parents are to tell them their kids are in trouble. How does that help? I'm sick of it. It's horrible. Yeah, well, "Your child, I found out that he or she stole from my classroom," or something. But it doesn't help. They should say, "I think maybe your kid might be experiencing some issues and that's why maybe they're failing their work. Is there anything . . . ?" They should recommend things to help. Maybe recommend a tutor. Actually involve yourself in the child's life, not just in the child's education.   ALMA

Before You Send a Student Out of Class Again
An Exercise for Teachers

When a middle school student acts up in class, what the teacher does in response can lay down a routine that easily turns into a habit. For example, if you send kids out of class for throwing spitballs (or refusing to do their work, or distracting others, or making inappropriate comments, or aggressive interactions), you teach them that such actions routinely result in leaving the classroom. But is there something more positive that you actually want your students to learn, or practice, as an alternative to behaving badly?

If you have asked a student to leave class, try answering these questions:

What did the student do? _____

_____

_____

What was happening just before the student acted this way? _____

_____

_____

As you think now about what was happening, can you see a purpose the student's behavior may be serving (e.g., to avoid a difficult task, to retaliate for a slight)? _____

_____

_____

What do you hope this student will do instead, the next time a similar situation arises? _____

_____

_____

_____

What does the student need to learn in order to respond in the way you hope?

_____

_____

_____

What can this student do *right now* that would give practice in the desired behavior? _____

_____

_____

What *next step* does the student need to take in learning or practicing the desired behavior? _____

_____

_____

What might you do to help the student take that next step? _____

_____

_____

KNOW EVERYTHING, SEE EVERYTHING

Working on issues of fairness with your students goes a long way toward helping them feel responsible for themselves and each other. Still, as middle schoolers experience the confusing pushes and pulls of their daily social interactions, they want and need your presence and your watchful eye.

They are continually exploring the boundary between what you see and hear, and what you don't.

> When the teacher's not watching, then the kids curse at each other or throw things. Then the teacher finds out about it, but she don't know who to blame, so she just blame everybody. So then everybody get in trouble. The people who did not do it should not get in trouble, but that's how people are. But I tell on people, 'cause I'm not getting in trouble for what I did not do.   THEA

> The teacher should know that when her back is turned, kids are making faces about her or talking about her. Then when they turn back around, we start acting like we wasn't doin' nothin'. I've done it myself sometimes. I got caught, but then I said I didn't do it, but the teacher knew I did it 'cause she seen me.   TATZI

They also know when you have heard or seen something but are pretending that you haven't. While you may choose not to react to every little indiscretion in order to keep your class going, you take risks when you "choose your battles." The most serious risk is that you will consistently overlook the behavior of some students, but not others.

> [My friend] found this wallet in the gym and stole it. I guess my teacher loves her still, but she found out how bad my friend really acts. She doesn't see the

masks [we hide behind] anymore. She's more aware. I'm thankful that there's a teacher like that. But not a lot of teachers are like that.   CARMELA

Teachers think that some people are star students, they're the best, they're really smart, they're just great. They don't know that outside of their classroom, they're swearing, doing other stuff that the teachers think are inappropriate. In my class, there was this one kid who was always smart, well behaved, and then outside the classroom he was always swearing, and doing bad stuff. I think they should know more about that.   DANIEL

Your students are practicing different roles in different places. They need you to help them sort out the many pressures that may interfere with their focus in the classroom.

In my class we've been going through so much trouble, 'cause of peer pressure. We started to have class discussions about problems and about things we see each other doing that we don't like to see each other doing. Even if it takes time off math, this is really important because teachers are the people who teach the students how to be when they grow up. The children are the future. We don't want our leaders in the future to be hypocrites. We don't want them to be confused. If we have leaders like that, think about how the followers will be!   CARMELA

Kids know that your presence in informal moments matters as much as your classroom role.

I just wish that there was a teacher during passing period that would stand outside and watch the hallway. 'Cause at my school there's a lot of fights.   EDWARD

Kids ask to use the bathroom and they don't really go to the bathroom, they wander around the hallway.   KATELIN

They count on you, since you know them already, to understand and to help them through difficult moments in the halls or on the playground. To help them out, first you have to see what is really happening.

The teachers should try to interact a little bit with the students, like during recess, even though the students may not like it. Teachers should really observe. Because it really helps. People are getting really touchy at my school, and sometimes people cover up for people so they can make out. A lot of the boys are really also, like, perverts there. They touch girls, and the girls, well, they're so used to it that they don't do anything about it. And everyone swears now. It's a habit. After every single frickin' word, they swear. It's very annoying.   CARMELA

By noticing the dynamics among kids outside the classroom—bullying, fighting, sexual harassment, profanity—you will not only keep kids safe from harm, you will also be responding to their need to have you understand what is going on.

Bullies don't pick on people bigger than them, they just pick on shrimpy little kids. You can see that they can't do anything back to the bullies. I feel like I should try to stand up for them, but then if I do, the bullies might beat me up. There could be a line of bullies and they try to chase you or beat you up, and you have to try to run away from them. I just walk away and if I see a teacher, I tell them.   EDWARD

Sometimes it's good for the teachers to step in, sometimes it's not. If a kid gets scared of something—if he's down, and you see him getting bullied— and then he walks over to a group or a teacher, then the teacher might know that he's getting bullied. Most of the kids that get picked on just ignore it. I don't think it's fun. JASON

All too often, the problems kids experience outside the classroom will also surface, in small ways, inside the classroom.

When we got a problem with a student [in class], teachers don't want to listen to it. They just be like, "Ignore it, ignore it." But you can't really ignore the problem that you having, and then you go to settle the problem and you all end up fighting. THEA

The time you take to work out such issues lets students see that the benefits of conflict resolution can carry over into the classroom, too.

On Thursdays, seventh-grade classes have this little extra section called "goal time" and we talk about little goals we want to accomplish in the class. Then my class has time for issues. Kids can say, "Oh, I have an issue with this person," and then they try to solve it right there. Everybody else in the class will listen and try to help, instead of just listening to the argument and gossiping. GENESIS

I had a problem with my best friend. She was getting jealous of me hanging out with her other best friend. So we had a fight, and the teacher talked to us, and how he settled it was kind of weird for me. We had to change our shoes and act like we were the other person, and that's how we settled our problems. She put on my shoes. Then, we had to pretend we were the other person and talk about why we might be mad at each other, and why were we sad, and what were we thinking. I was shy at first. I've never settled something before like that. Then we started being friends again, and I want to be thankful for that.   JESSICA

Jessica is not alone in feeling relieved and grateful. Once you hear what students say about the social obstacles that keep them from learning, you will find many strategies to address those issues. Along the way, you are likely to see students relax and blossom in the classroom, developing the social habits that support their academic skills and understanding.

In the next chapter, students describe how a teacher's individual interactions with them can support and guide them to take up those tasks.

SUMMARY
Social Forces in the Classroom

- Help us find common ground with each other.
- Teach us how to work together in safe, collaborative groups.
- Let us practice working out issues that affect the class.
- Treat us all with the same respect.
- Understand that our ideas about what's fair will change as we tackle new problems.
- Watch closely what's really going on with us, inside and outside the classroom.

CHAPTER 4

Helping Us Grow into Confident Learners

"Sometimes I want to ask the question, but I don't want to seem like I'm dumb."

How they are doing in school affects middle school students' sense of themselves. They are newly able to measure themselves through the eyes of others, their peers, and their teachers. They are eager to feel confident, even when they feel out of balance in the rest of their lives. They want their teachers to stick with them, to help them feel successful even when they don't yet know if they can be.

> I had a lot of dramatic things happen to me in the eighth grade. I was really bitter. My math teacher was very helpful; he made a big impact on my personality. He pushed us and pushed us, and if you needed help, he'd take his lunch break off and teach it to you a million times until you got it. By the end of the year, I got that I had to study. But he was also very funny. If we were having a bad day, or if you looked like you were really sad, he would find a way to make us feel better. He had a Barney on his shelf, and he

would put it on our desk and no matter how much of a bad mood you're in, as soon as you look at it, you start smiling.   HEATHER

In every interaction kids have with you and the school, they are looking for information about themselves as learners. Whether from classroom placements or offhand remarks, they often draw conclusions that discourage them.

I feel dumb, I feel bad inside, because they put the other people in smarter classes. They're putting them way over there, and they're smarter than me, but we're both [learning] the same skills and we're both getting the same grade. It makes me feel different.   TIFFANY

One thing that makes me feel kind of dumb is when the teacher acts sarcastic with you, like if you say something that you think is correct and she just says, "Oh yeah, that's correct"—and then goes, "Not."   CANEK

Tiffany and Canek remind us that keeping vulnerable middle school students engaged in learning depends on their good relationship with their teachers. In elementary school, we take for granted that the student-teacher relationship matters. In the middle grades, it's easy to shift the focus onto academics alone—and to consider the social aspects of their learning as secondary.

However, as students told us in chapter 2, kids in these years are newly sensitive to the tone and content of the teacher's personal interactions with them. Sarcasm, patronizing remarks, and other such interchanges will have a significant negative effect on what academic content they learn and how they learn it—especially for those students who already find school difficult. Your positive approach will help them thrive academically.

Even if it's in math class, you can see when somebody's insecure about themselves. You can see how they present themselves, what their work is

reasons the phrase "3 dummies" should NEVER come out of your mouth

LOOKING AT YOU NICCUM

like. If the teacher really cares about the students, they find some spare time and actually talk to the students, and make the student feel more comfortable. Find things that are good about the student.   ALMA

I had a really cool math teacher in eighth grade. Her name was Miss Butts, all right? Right off in the beginning, she'd get everything out of the way: "Yeah, my name is Miss Butts. You can laugh at it now." You could talk to her about anything, and she'd usually lead you in a good way, she wouldn't tell her advice on it first. She'd help you a lot on math. I really got it.   KAITLYN

Whatever issues kids are struggling with, your attentiveness will give support to them in both the personal and the academic challenges of learning.

My eighth-grade English teacher was somebody that you could really talk to and tell your problems to, and she would keep it to herself. If you were sad, she'd crack jokes and try to make you happy, and she always would play around with you. But she was a really good teacher. Her class wasn't really that hard. She would break it down, till you understood what she was trying to teach you.   VERONICA

My math teacher was always there when I needed help. He's just really a nice person. He's a preacher too. He can really connect with people—if he wants to know what's wrong with you, he tells you what's wrong with *him,* and so you tell him back, so you won't feel left out. I asked him anything and he would always tell me. Sometimes we played chess; he's a real good chess player. He showed me step by step every problem and how to do it, and how everything went. I feel like I'm doing better 'cause of him. He taught me everything I really knew about math. I was one of the people in his class to actually pay attention. When I get older I want to be a math teacher.   BRANDON

I would legit cry if one of my students told me they wanted to be a teacher

Tracking: Sort Us or Teach Us Together?

Like their teachers, middle school students are divided on the issue of ability grouping. Whichever side they take, however, they cast it as a fairness issue. Some representative comments from students on the subject:

Sort Us

It would be better if they made our classes longer and got into better discussions, not just, "Oh here's your notes, write them down." If they raised the level a little bit. I know we've got people from all different levels, but for the people that are on a higher level, the work is easy. For the people that are struggling, I understand, but they're holding us back.   RACHELL

I wish they could make it more interesting for us. They still give

Teach Us Together

If you get [the lowest grade on the test], you go to the "one" class. There they tell you something once—so if you don't get it that once, you don't belong in that class. In the "two" class, they repeat you two times. But we're learning the same thing. So what's the point of this one, two, three, and four, when we're going to learn the same thing? It makes me feel dumb. What I want, in my opinion, is to stuff everybody in the classroom and just teach them together.   DIANA

The problem here is less than ideal teaching/differentiation not that you should be tracked me work that's like retaking the last grade over again. I think they should put us in different categories, so we can all move ahead and become better people, but we wouldn't be holding anybody back or pushing anybody behind. 'Cause I'm ahead of some people and I might be behind some people.   KAITLYN

Kids who don't pay attention, or act rude, send them to a different class—or a different school. There's a "bad" school [for those students].   ERIC F.

I agree with Diana: If I could stuff three hundred students in one classroom, I would, and I would teach them—I would have four teachers helping me, if I could. But unfortunately, I can't, and we got to go by grades.   TIFFANY

I disagree with Eric. I don't think we should have to go to a different school if we're not paying attention. I know sometimes *he* don't be paying attention in class. Does that mean he should go to a different school?   AMANDA N.

HELP WHEN KIDS NEED IT

Students want you to care about them as people, and to reach out to them when they most need you. Amanda's teacher, for example, gave each student a journal and responded to their entries day by day.

to everyone every day?
HOW? THAT'S LIKE 150 notes
EVERY DAY

If we had a problem or something, we could tell her and she'd write back and give us the best advice she could. If we missed a lot of school, she'd be there to help us; she'd try to get us all caught up with our subjects before our final grades were due. It pushed me to where I figured I needed to come to school more, so that I wouldn't have all that work at one time. I'd be a little more independent than what I was.   AMANDA S.

Chanté believes that two particular teachers helped her make it from sixth to eighth grade, both personally and academically.

They basically set me down, one on one. If I'm struggling in math, she keeps me and works with me and helps me more, so when I head to high school I won't struggle in math. Ever since she helping me one on one, I'm starting to understand math now. One of my teachers was very strict on me. Every time I get mad over something, she pulls me out in the hallway and tries to calm me down, and basically talks to me about controlling my temper and staying on task with my work.   CHANTÉ

Some of the ways kids will call on you for help may be unexpected, but they are taking you at your word.

A lot of teachers say they're there for you, but a lot of times, they're just saying that, to seem like a good teacher. Then they turn out to be totally different. At the beginning of the year, a teacher said: "If you have any problems, you can tell me and I'll help you." I didn't know who was going to pick me up, I wasn't sure if I could stay there for a long time, and I asked him, "Can I use your phone?" and he said no. I said, "How am I going to get home?" They think they know what you're going through, but then they have no idea. They assume things.   GENESIS

When you help them in the ways they need and ask for, when you reach out to students in small ways that seem to have nothing to do with academic matters, you lay the groundwork for something very important in the classroom: their belief that you will support them in their learning, whatever stands in its way.

GETTING THINGS WRONG, GETTING THINGS RIGHT

Students in the middle grades want to be able to learn from their mistakes. But being wrong often feels like being stupid, especially if it happens in public or if negative consequences follow.

> Teachers say it's okay to raise your hand. Sometimes I want to ask the question, but I don't want to seem like I'm dumb. Or I'm not sure if the teacher said it already, and I don't want to get the teacher on the wrong side. GABE

Teachers may respond in ways that inadvertently play into students' fears of ridicule.

> When you raise your hand and the teacher calls on you, [sometimes] you suddenly forget what you're going to say and the teacher's, like, "If you have nothing to say, don't say it." DANIEL

Kids sometimes step in to rescue each other, but such situations can leave them feeling reluctant to risk engagement later.

> I don't like when teachers put people on the spot. If the teacher calls on somebody and they're not ready or they're totally lost, somebody else will jump in for them, kind of in an indirect way, and help the person. I do this, and my friends do it sometimes for me. ALMA

Middle schoolers realize that their academic work is now more difficult than it was in elementary school. They want clear and forthright communication from you, letting them know whether they understand or misunderstand the material. They need you to convey that information in a way that does not feel patronizing.

When a teacher calls on you and when you're talking they're like, "Right, right." Then if you say something wrong, the teacher's like, "That's right, that's right, but I'm not looking for that." Tell me if it's wrong or not, you know? They act like they just don't want to make you feel bad, and that kind of babies you. You don't want them to tell you you're doing bad—but you don't want them to tell you you're really good, when you're not. When you're little, if you do a dance, even if you fall your parents or teachers still clap, like, "Wow, that's amazing," and they don't criticize you. Well, the older you get, I think it's time for constructive criticism. I hate it when teachers are fake—if the picture's really ugly: "Oh, it's so amazing." You know it's not, you can see. Don't pretend like it is.   ALMA

(handwritten margin note: BE AUTHENTIC / respond positively / And authentically)

MAKE IT HARD AND SHOW US HOW TO DO IT

When the teacher finds ways to help the entire class succeed, students feel safer asking questions and getting help. If you let them believe that being confused is an individual problem, then they are more likely to withdraw than to ask a question.

My teacher encouraged everyone, and everybody liked her—everyone strived to do well in her class, because they wanted to get on her good side. She could be strict, but she knew how to handle kids well. She would give you one day to do math and if you had questions, you would write a question mark and she would go over it in class. And she'd give you two days to do science. If we had a question she would always be around and we could always ask her questions and she would always try and help us do well in class.   ITAI

But for a student who is not succeeding, taking them aside privately can make all the difference. Your confidence that they can do better helps kids believe in themselves, too.

I didn't really like science, but that was sometimes because I didn't know what I had to do. I tried not to participate, 'cause I'm shy when I really don't know something. But the science teacher, one time he kept me after school. I thought it was for a bad reason, but he just wanted to talk to me. He wanted to get me more involved and he said that he knew I could be outspoken and participate, if I just knew what I was doing. So he helped me. It made me feel like I knew what I was doing, and I just started to get more ideas. When my team didn't come up with anything, I would have an idea and just tell them, and we'd end up doing it. Sometimes it would work, sometimes it wouldn't. After a while, I started to like that class.   KENSON

Using "brainstorming" techniques, as Kenson's teacher does, taps into students' natural desire to talk to each other and encourages creative thinking and enthusiasm while allowing the students to build on the ideas of others. But for brainstorming to be effective, you need to be alert to the obstacles some students will face, and, like Kenson's teacher, you may need to address them out of the public eye.

Another teacher devised a way to spark students' creative ideas about testing their own knowledge of history.

> My history teacher wants to see what we want to learn. One whole period, she let us make up what we wanted on a test. Say somebody wanted a crossword, they would have to make the crossword, and then she would put one on the test. It was our idea, but we gave it to her, and she gave the student credit who made up the idea. KENSON

Kids want your acknowledgment and encouragement when they have a good idea or finally get something right.

> [It makes you feel smart] when teachers become enthusiastic about you getting the correct answer. CARMELA

> [I like it] if teachers do something a little bit extra, not just, "Okay, that's the correct answer," but if they write you a note or a comment like, "That's really good, you've been studying." ALMA

> I got a 60 on my test, and my teacher said that if I do my homework and get good grades on my homework, I can get my grades raised up. KATELIN

At the same time, they dislike it when you single students out for public praise. It helps to stay away from terms like "best" and "most."

[handwritten margin note: Duh?? don't pit kids against other?!]

> I think everyone should be praised for something they do. A lot of teachers single students out. To say, "Good job, your work is amazing, you're the best student in this class," that wouldn't be right. It kind of puts our hopes down, like, "Uhh, I might as well not even try." You just kind of give up on yourself. ALMA

In science class there's a really smart guy, he always gets 100 on his work. The teacher says, "Oh, you're smarter than me," and stuff. Everyone can do well, but we don't want the teacher to brag about people, 'cause that'll make everyone else feel dumb and stupid. If you're too smart, people make fun of you, like you're a nerd.   EDWARD

Middle schoolers need both your challenge *and* your support. Tiffany says she would be more interested in Egypt if her teacher connected the class material to the things she knows and enjoys.

A boring teacher doesn't have actions to what he or she reads or says. She comes in and says, "Turn to page seventeen, start reading it, and write a paragraph about what is a fact." You got to make it fun, like: "Today, we're going to do ancient Egypt. We're going to write about what happened back then. How they used to build their homes and what they used to eat." And then tell you, "Just get working and then we'll read it all as a group and then share our answers."   TIFFANY

You can pose learning tasks that are just out of reach, and let students grapple with them for a while. But at a certain point, they will need you to step in to offer guidance.

My English teacher in eighth grade made a big impact on me, even though she was my least favorite teacher. I didn't know how to study in eighth grade, I just never studied. But once I experienced about a month in her class, I knew I had to study for all my spelling and vocabulary tests. She just gave us an assignment, she didn't teach it. If we asked a question, she didn't answer it. She made us teach ourselves, in a way. Then at the end, if everybody was doing horribly, she'd come and teach it to us, and ask for questions.   HEATHER

Offering students lots of practice with the new skills they are learning also communicates your belief that in time they will get it right.

> The way the teachers teach, that's what made me want to act more mature. I can remember my [English] teacher in eighth grade. He stayed on us about doing our essays and stuff. Nobody liked essays, but now it's my favorite subject. Writing an essay. I could write one in about five minutes, because he taught us the formula so many times, really trying to get it across. BRIAN

They appreciate your clear and candid feedback, but they need it to come in the friendly tone of a good coach.

> In middle school I had a math teacher and she wouldn't sugarcoat it for people. She would actually sit you down to look at all your grades, and show you what would happen. She would bring you down to reality, give you the straightforward of what would be the end result. But the way she would speak about it, you wouldn't be hurt or offended, you'd have a good mindset. GEOFFERY

You can also support your students' learning through the mistakes they make. If you maintain an encouraging stance, they will find it easier to accept your corrections.

> When you learn from your mistakes, you find a way to do something better. If you get something wrong, a teacher could just explain to you why it's wrong and why what she's saying is correct. CANEK

> I'm not scared about my mistakes. A lot of people are, and I think that it's something they have to get over, and just realize, "I will have a lot of

mistakes." It's the teacher's job to give them constructive criticism of what they can do. I've known some teachers who do that.   ALMA

A climate of "learning from mistakes" will develop in your classroom as you yourself acknowledge your mistakes, admit what you don't know, and tell the students what you wonder about. When you say, "Oops, I made a mistake, let's try again!" students hear, "It's okay to make mistakes as long as you correct them."

Kids need to hear your honest and specific appraisal of what they do well on a regular basis, and not just what they still need to work on.

I had a paper graded and they just marked the bad stuff and didn't point out the good stuff that I wrote. It just made me feel bad about myself. Teachers should say something positive to motivate the student to do better. When they correct papers they always mark the stuff that's wrong, and just say, "Improve on that, fix that." They should say some stuff that will help the student feel better about themselves.   DANIEL

Middle schoolers won't necessarily see their mistakes as an opportunity for learning new skills and information. They are just as likely to interpret your corrections as a critical judgment about themselves. Simply not knowing how to do something makes them feel vulnerable. So how you approach them makes a big difference in terms of whether or not they can hear and understand what you're saying.

If you're struggling in a class, the teacher should come up and ask if you two [student and teacher] can work on something, so that you can improve. It's easier for me to do one-on-ones, so I can ask as much questions as I'd like without worrying about being embarrassed, or looking at the clock. It's really important for the teacher to tell the student that the student isn't dumb, other kids are struggling also. It's good to repeat [those] things that you should remember, even though it might be annoying. CARMELA

When they don't understand something in class, for example, kids may not ask for your help directly. Instead, they might do something to gain the attention—and, they hope, the respect—of their peers, even if it means getting in trouble with you. When you need to intervene in disruptive classroom behavior, striking the right tone will help students refocus on their work without losing face.

The teachers who showed that they cared, they didn't just want to send you out of the class for petty stuff. They'll maybe send you out one time, and then they'll sit you down after class and talk to you about the problem that occurred in class. [Learning] is not about playing. It's about coming to school and doing your work. [So it's] not only being nice, it's staying on me about my work too. Staying on everybody about their work. Making sure everybody doing the same thing. Ain't no lollygagging. It's time to wake up and smell the coffee. BRIAN

Your students want you to keep the classroom a serious place for learning, because they can't always do it themselves. When they do act up, they want you to deal with them in a respectful way, and then help them refocus.

HOW GRADES AFFECT KIDS

As students approach the end of the middle grades, they may begin to understand the ways teachers use grades both to assess their work and to encourage them to do better.

When you get a bad grade and teachers say you're trying, I think they're just trying to motivate you to study next time, and try harder to get that A or B that you want.   DANIEL

I don't think they'll say that you're something that you're not. A kid can be good at math and get a C. That's still possible. The teachers, they'll say that to encourage you to do better, 'cause the teachers know what you can do and what you can't, and the teachers want to make you learn.   CARMELA

But many students will experience your encouragement as contradicting the grade you assign—and when that happens, they listen to the grade.

At my school, teachers say stuff when it's not true. Like they say you're good at math just because you try, even though you just got a bad grade. So people don't really listen to what the teachers say now, 'cause it's not true.   EDWARD

They don't always try to help us on everything. They try to criticize us as we go do our work, and as we get a low grade. "Why did you get a low grade? Did you study?" Yes, I did study—but we don't always get the problems.   SHANIECE

When their grade does not affirm their effort, students may be quick to give up on taking risks and will lose interest in the learning itself. If you try to use grades to motivate students, it may succeed with the ablest students in your class, but many others, like Shaniece, will be left feeling discouraged.

Students are sensitive to how they stand compared to other students in their class. Whether they get good grades or poor grades, they don't want to call attention to them.

Another Way You Judge Us: How Standardized Tests Feel to Kids

Even when teachers try to minimize the importance of standardized testing, middle school students still feel as though the tests are judging them personally. This raises their anxiety at the same time that it taps into their strong beliefs about fairness.

> They shouldn't criticize the children, because it's not our fault what we're not learning what's on the test. My friend's school teaches a lot of stuff and gives a lot of homework, so they learn more. The school I go to takes forever to explain stuff on one page. They don't teach that well. If they gave tests based on what you learn, that would be a good judgment. If they give stuff based on what they think you should know, I don't think that's right. AMELIA

> Kids may know something, but they tend to forget when they're nervous. Sometimes when I take a test, maybe I forget at that moment, but after the test, it might just come right off my hand. It depends on how you feel that day. KENSON

> During a test, you get so nervous and you lose everything, it's just a little weird. Because once you're done with it, you can say, "Oh, I remember that," but you can't go back to those tests that you've taken. I think they should just use your regular testing from school. JAVIER

If you don't know a word on the test, they're not even allowed to tell you what the word means! If a question really revolves around that one word, you can't really answer it to your fullest ability.   DAQUAN

There was a question that we hadn't even learned yet, and I was a little confused. The teacher said, "Oh, don't worry about it—just take a wild guess because we haven't talked about it." I'm not going to take a wild guess, because this affects me, and it affects what the state is going to know about me. The teacher said, "It's my fault that I haven't taught you this yet," but I said, "Well, you should prepare us for what's going to happen."   JAVIER

It doesn't make sense. They base everything on how you do on testing, like what high school might want [from] you when you get older. What if you don't do so good, but you're really, really smart?   KENSON

I think the teacher should [give criticism] privately, 'cause kids make fun of you when you don't do good—they call you dumb and stupid. I usually go check my grade after school, so I'm by myself and no one's going to hear it.   EDWARD

I don't like people getting on my case. If I get A's and they get D's, I don't really care if I get made fun of, but it's just annoying. Or if I get a C they'll be like "You got a C? Omigod, the smartest person got a C!" They'll be spreading it around. It should be private. It's my information, my information only. I'll share it with you if you really want to know, but why should you know?   CARMELA

You may want to give feedback on how the whole class did, as a way of encouraging students to do better. But take care not to reveal a student's grade, which is private information.

Instead of reading down a list, "This person got 90 percent," a teacher could say a quick general thing: "Some people did excellent, some people did well, some people didn't do so well." So the people who didn't do so well will try harder next time.   GABE

Grades may matter to your students' parents in ways that you never intended. They may believe that a good student always gets a top grade. They may reward or punish children for their grades. Whatever the situation, students will have to try to balance their parents' concerns, their own, and yours.

I'm always trying to get A's, trying to please my mom because I know she has a lot on her mind, and if I get bad grades, then it's just another problem for her to deal with. So my first-quarter report card [in sixth grade] was all A's, and I wanted to keep that up. Then [later] my science grade was a B. "No, I have to get an A, is there anything I can do to bring that up?" My sixth-grade teacher was really nice. She said, "Okay, we can do something." So we had to do a project for the science fair and that's what brought my grade up to an A. I really appreciate it, because not all teachers would let you bring your grade up even though it was already good.   GENESIS

We further explore the subject of parents' responses to students' grades in chapter 6 ("Make Way for Parents").

How Do I Grade?
An Exercise for Teachers

How you go about grading can contribute substantially to how confident students feel in your class, to how well they learn from mistakes, and to how they feel about the subject you teach. For many students, this will be their first experience with real grades.

Before you give grades, ask yourself the following questions, also noting any reflections or new ideas you have about your practices:

Why am I grading students on this assignment? _____

_____

_____

Have I clearly stated (in discussions and in assessment rubrics) what grading system I use and what each grade means? _____

How do I use ungraded pre-assessments? (Check all that apply.)

___ To help students identify what they already know and can do

___ To help me identify their misconceptions

___ To let students pose their own questions about a new subject area

___ To let students know where they are going (what the learning goals are)

When I grade student work, do students see what they got right and where they still need to improve? _____

How do I grade something other than a test or quiz (such as a project, an oral presentation, or a research paper)? (Check all that apply.)

___ I use a common rubric for students, even when I offer them a range of choices about how to demonstrate their learning.

_____ I provide feedback early and often, so that students can use my grading criteria to guide them while the work is still in process.

_____ Students have opportunities to see and talk about their ongoing work, using the grading criteria I have created. (Students assess their own work and/or give feedback to each other.)

_____ I clearly state how students can revise their work or improve their grade in other ways.

What other forms of evaluation do I give to students, besides a letter grade? Do my students understand how those other evaluations connect to the grades I give them?

_____

_____

_____

After reading your answers above, write down any reflections and new ideas:

_____

_____

_____

HOW TO HELP KIDS LEARN

Your supportive attitude in the classroom will show up in many different ways. In the following pages, middle schoolers offer their best ideas for how teachers could help them do better in school.

Keep it simple. Focus your help on a specific goal or task.

I think that teachers should help you with the problem. If you get a C in English, then they should help you with what you need help on. That's how the teachers can actually help you. JESSICA

Sometimes they give us an example of a small problem and then they skip through to a bigger problem. I think they should just take it step by step, until we understand that, and then give harder and harder problems. GENESIS

Support us in mastering the new vocabulary of our subjects.

For me, life science is my hardest subject, because science has all those big difficult words and our teachers make you memorize the definitions—like osmosis, and different parts of the cells, the nucleus, and the "nucleo-lus." It's hard to get all those long definitions for those big words in my brain—those two words look exactly the same, and sometimes I forget. They give you a test the following week. She should cut down on the words. Instead of giving us ten words, she could make it half that. DENUE

My English teacher, she's giving us good tips. She's said, "This one will be on the test." She gave us a definition for it, and when I saw that on the test I automatically knew what it was.   KENSON

Use different strategies to help us learn.

Try to show kids their own way of learning. Like my way of learning, I have to see or touch things to learn. Some people have to hear things.   AMANDA N.

Teachers should make a phrase sometimes for us to learn things. Like in math here, "Please Excuse My Dear Aunt Sally," P-E-M-D-A-S, it's supposed to be about order of operations. That helps you learn—like when you come back to [a problem] you can think in your head, "What does P stand for?"   GABE

Help us get organized, and tell us why it matters.

If I don't keep my stuff organized, my teacher makes me miss ten minutes of recess, and we only have twenty minutes of recess, so that really stinks. If you're not organized, it's no fun and you can't find anything when you need it. So now I have a really thick binder with different sections. I can keep all my work in it and when I need it, I just open up to that section. Once a week [it helps to have] a binder check. You get a check minus or a check plus, depending on what condition your binder is in.   DAQUAN

It is helpful if they give you more advice on how to get organized better. I was very disorganized. As soon as my adviser did binder-check on me, all my papers fell out, and I tried to stuff them back in. He had a talk with my mom about this. He took away my recess, so we could go over organization and it really helped.   JAVIER

Every Friday, my teacher would give us back work that we had done, and we wouldn't really need it. We already knew what our grade was, and we would ask her if we could just recycle it or bring it home. "No, you have to keep it." Then it's just more and more papers in your backpack and your binder and you don't know what to do with it. Why are we keeping our stuff organized?   GENESIS

Coordinate homework assignments and tests with other teachers.

I'm bringing it straight out, they shouldn't give that much homework. 'Cause we have so many classes and they give so much homework. Sometimes we focus on one class and not so much on another, and we have a pop quiz [on things] we won't know, and we'll get bad grades. We have so much homework to do, we have no time to go places or do things we have to do at home. Personal stuff, or maybe sometimes you want time to go outside or whatever.   ERIC F.

We have seven classes a day, and they give three or four pieces of homework, sometimes front and back. That's a lot of homework to be doing. When we get to [the after-school program], it's like 3:15, so we only have till 4:30. It's not enough time for us to do all seven classes' homework.   KATELIN

Help us help each other to get our homework done.

My mom and I were talking about a buddy system, so if you didn't want to do your homework, you would be paired up with someone. Someone would call you every night and tell you, "Don't forget to do this project," or "Did you do your homework?" If you say no, "Well, then, why not?" My friend and I, we check on each other sometimes. If we have a problem we can't figure out, we try and figure it out together, or if I need something, I call her.   ITAI

Give us time in school to do homework and get help on it.

You have to give the kids time to study. You have to go over the stuff so the kids will know what to do.   EDWARD

I don't like American history that much, and I have to do this project and I don't understand how, except the bibliography. If you want to get help, you go to the homeroom teacher, 'cause they know your whole schedule and they see your homework in the morning. It's not hard for me to ask for help, but it's hard for me to get it done when I also have other homework and things to do. I wait till the last three days, 'cause projects are due two weeks apart. The homeroom teacher was talking to my friend, saying that "You should do reports over the weekend—do one project one weekend, and skip the next weekend [while you do another one]." But I would rather do the same project until it's done, and then do the other project right after.   JASON

Use your calls home to support us.

I would really, really like it if my teacher would sometimes call home for a good thing that I do. My dad never seems to realize any good thing that I do, it's like he's blind. He pressures me on the bad things that I do. It's like he takes a list and he counts up all the bad things. So if my teacher, instead of calling home whenever I do a bad thing, she would sometimes call home when I do a good thing, and let my dad know that I actually try hard, then I would do better.   AMELIA

Maybe the teacher could call home to say, "Oh, your son or daughter seems to be distracted or disturbed by something," to find out what's happening. If the parents are acting ignorant and rude, you figure maybe that the student is having a hard time at home.   KENSON

Ask for our feedback.

There's not an ideal, perfect teacher. So teachers should maybe take a survey, like a quarter of the way through the semester. "How's my class going? Is homework taking too long? Are you getting stressed out? Should I explain things more clearly? How can I make you a better student, or how can I help you learn better, or how can I help your attitude?" Just so students can tell them what to improve on and what was good.   GABE

TALK ABOUT KIDS' ISSUES, TOO

When they trust you, middle schoolers want opportunities to discuss with you the personal and social issues they face as early adolescents. Whether these conversations take place in health, social studies, or English classes, advisory or academic support groups, or other group settings, kids gain more than just content knowledge from them. As you engage students in thinking about the changes and choices they face, they will learn to communicate better and to reason things through with greater thoughtfulness.

I think there should be classes teaching the students about themselves, like about sex ed, about smoking, about drugs, but also about moral values. About who you are and who you want to be when you grow up. What you're going to do. Because a lot of people are confused about who they really are.   CARMELA

Students perceive teachers as reluctant to have these discussions with them. (Sometimes they are correct, as many schools have strict policies about health education.) They will make up their own theories about why you are reluctant, however.

Teachers are scared to talk about sex and stuff. Not many of the teachers talk about it, cause I think they're shy about that topic or something. They talk about other stuff, but they don't talk about sex, I don't know why. It would be better if they weren't as shy. They can be honest with you on things like that.   EDWARD

You start learning about your health, like about sex, about drugs, about alcohol. And peer pressure—the pressure to do something is there. A lot of times teachers are not comfortable talking about that. One of the mistakes teachers make: They talk about it, but they don't tell you what it *is*. They just say, "Don't do it. It's bad for you." *Why* is it bad for you?   ALMA

But when you are willing to listen, kids will have all kinds of questions to ask.

One day of the week they take one period, and a teacher comes and actually talks to you about things that are happening in the streets. She gives you a skills book you can write in; it's yours to keep. It has questions about things you shouldn't do: "Should you sell drugs in the street?" and you've got to explain why the answer would be no, why it would be bad for you. It's kind of interesting, because you learn things that are happening, and why you should not do drugs, not smoke. Why you should be in school and learn and do your work. I liked it. I actually learned things and I'm glad I know them, but I felt weird.   TIFFANY

If you approach such conversations without assuming things about your students, they give you a glimpse of the actual circumstances of their lives.

I don't think the teachers know that a lot of the students have gone through a lot of things. A lot of the students have issues, like they either don't know a parent, or their parents are separated, or a lot of people that they know have died. I don't think the teachers know that most of the students really know about sex ed and really know about the outside world. I think the teachers think we have virgin ears. But we don't. I think in a way, we almost live—some of us, or most of us—an adult life. Almost. Not really. But we can peek into it a little bit.   CARMELA

WHEN TROUBLE PULLS KIDS DOWN

Sometimes a student does not thrive in your classroom, even when you give your best efforts in support. Their problems may be too big for you to handle on your own. If, when you express concern, students respond to your caring questions by revealing serious personal issues they are facing, talk with someone else at the school—the counselor, the nurse, the principal—who is in a position to help. Such counseling goes beyond your responsibility.

> The counselors sometimes help, but most of the kids who need a lot of help don't talk about it [to teachers]. If I'm a kid on the street and you ask me, I'm not going to sit there telling you that I'm on drugs and my mom's in jail and my dad just shot a dude. I'm not going to feel comfortable to tell you that. But you can find another way to know, without letting me know, and just help me. I would feel like you don't pity me, but you actually care about me.   AMELIA

> You can tell when a kid is depressed, or you know there's something going on. You don't have to actually ask him, but you know when is the right time to butt in. Sometimes, you can ask one of the kid's closest friends, because kids are very close and they tell each other everything, or they could witness it. They'll tell you, but they'll probably also talk to their friend about it and say, "Maybe you should talk to the teacher, maybe she can help you." I think that's a good way to reach out to the child.   JAVIER

Above all, when students are tackling the newly challenging middle school curriculum, they need to believe that they *can* do it. By sticking with them and supporting them through discouraging times, you are helping them not to give up.

But providing academic challenges and supports will not accomplish your classroom goals unless students are paying attention. In the next chapter, students talk about how you might help them manage their energies and focus on their tasks.

SUMMARY
Helping Us Grow into Confident Learners

- Realize that what you say to us helps us decide whether we believe we are smart or not.
- Listen to our opinions about how you teach us.
- Give us friendly and honest feedback on what we do right and what we need to do better.
- Communicate your confidence in us as you help us overcome our struggles in school.
- Understand that the grades you give us may mean different things to you, to us, and to our parents.
- Help us learn how to manage our homework.

CHAPTER 5

Using Our Energy to Help Us Learn

"It's not going to be boring because you'll be doing something that you like to do."

Even when they come to you eager to learn and ready to work, students in the middle grades are still learning to manage their attention and energy in the classroom. They will run into problems if you ask them to "sit still and pay attention" for extended periods of time—instructions that are contradictory for students this age.

> We're ready to do something and the teachers are giving us work, and we just want to get out. That's what happens to me. I can't concentrate, I'm too hyper. I don't know how to get my energy out.   GABE

As kids' attention wanders, their restless energy goes up. Just as they have a hard time sustaining their attention, they also have trouble keeping their energies in check.

When you vary what you do in class, however, the focus of middle schoolers takes a turn for the better. Like all of us, students are better able to harness their attention and energy when they find the work—both what they do and how they do it—appealing.

GIVE KIDS A BREAK

Middle school students confined to their desks soon start to feel physical and mental signals that they need to move. Boys often feel this torment most keenly.

> If you had a test and then you have another test, through all your classes, you're going to be overloaded with all this. I get stressed out. I feel like I want to let my anger out, just do something to let it out. But I can't, 'cause I have to contain myself in class, so it's really hard. GABE

> Teachers should take things serious, but not very serious. They should let the kids have some free time once in a while and just do fun things. 'Cause if you just study the whole year, it's going to get like, "Whoa." It's stressful. After being in class a couple of hours, you need to have a break in the yard and play on the structure and play some ball. I sometimes get a headache. I feel like there's too much stuff in my head and it's going to blow up. EDWARD

When girls seek relief from the tedium of their studies, they may not need as much running around as boys do. Often they are looking for more social or interpersonal diversions.

> It's like we in school just to work all day and then go home. We got these bells and we have to go straight to class. If you be late then you get a lunch detention; if you get three tardies you get an after-school detention. You

don't have no time to talk. Even at lunch, you got to sit with the class you already have. But what if your best friend or your friend in the other class? You can't sit with them, so you don't really have nowhere to talk. We have I guess two or three minutes for passing to our next class, but that's not long. I would leave four minutes. Just give us a little bit more time, so we could say hi and conversate for a minute.   THEA

Tatzi also wants some time with her friends at school, just as she thinks her teachers have. She resists the constraints of lunchroom schedules and table assignments.

Lunch should be our free time. Teachers are getting their time off at lunch, so why can't we get our time off to do what we want to do?   TATZI

Social interactions can take place between students and teacher, as well. Kids like the break from your instruction, but they don't need it to dominate class time.

She used to tell us some of her dog stories, ten or fifteen minutes before the period: "This morning, I was going to take my dog out for a walk, and my dog went under the bed, and there was a mess, and I had to pull him out of the bed because he didn't want to go." During class, sometimes, when we're working independently and we finish our work after sharing, we have a little joke time.   DIANA

After they have been working for a sustained period in class, kids appreciate some time for fun.

My teachers make it fun, too. My math teacher, he tries everything. It might still be boring but at the end, we'll have music. Or today, we got through our math class and we all behaved, and so then we just had fun, like a paper fight with rolled-up paper.   JESSICA

To help them maintain their focus during "boring" instruction, you might post the day's agenda on the board, so they know another activity will be coming up later.

STOP BEFORE IT'S TOO MUCH

When you are explaining class material to your students, try to plan some variety in what you say and how you say it. Like Goldilocks in the house of the three bears, students don't want too little direct instruction and they don't want too much—just the right amount. This would be easier, of course, if "just right" were the same for each of them.

Many students would prefer to find out things themselves, rather than have the teacher explain it to them at length.

My teacher, he's a nice guy, but he keeps on explaining stuff when we *get* it. Like, talking about the parts of a microscope: "When you look through the eyepiece, there is a glass and you see the object." Why are you explaining this, we know that it's there!   GENESIS

Even the best-intended attempt to make a subject interesting will fall flat with students if all they hear is talk.

My math teacher also explains, but she'll get off topic. Like she gave us this homework about daily things that we wouldn't pay attention to, and the question went, "How many sides does a stop sign have?" Instead of just telling us that it has eight, she went into this stuff about that it has eight sides because somebody could be color blind, or not know how to read. She would let people give examples, and the examples would take forever, and then finally, we would move on. For me, math is really boring, and if she explains it, it's making the class even more boring.   GENESIS

Too little information from the teacher can also make kids uncomfortable, however. If they miss something, they may not have a way to ask without losing face.

Teachers think that since you're in honors, you're so smart. But sometimes things fill your mind, or you're spaced out in class. Then they get mad cause they think we're supposed to be perfect and be better than the normal kids—that's what they call the non-honors kids at our school. I think it's good to repeat things so that it gets sunk in kids' heads, so that they maybe won't forget.   GABE

For kids to stay attentive and also use their boundless energy, they need variety both in your instructional activities and in the pace of your instruction. You will find many ways to build such variety into their days, including creating collaborative learning and peer teaching activities. In the following pages, students describe some of these, here grouped into two important categories: activities that support their learning and activities that regulate their physical energies.

TEACH THROUGH ACTION

Kids like it when you enliven an academic lesson with playful learning strategies. For this to succeed, however, you will have to clearly tie the fun to your learning objectives. Otherwise, students will feel that you are simply treating them like little kids.

> Just letting us have fun, like playing games in class, is not necessarily respecting us. It's respect when we know that we have *done* something—like when games help us learn.   GENESIS

Adding an element of performance to your presentations will stimulate students' interest while also helping them sustain their attention and energy.

> Instead of just talking straight about a boring lesson, teachers could try to make it a little more fun and interesting. My sixth-grade math teacher would make a lot of little squeaky voices while she was explaining, or start a little story to make us remember. She would make up little funny songs about math.   JAVIER

Music and physical movement in a lesson create an information-rich memory of what you want students to know, and allows them to access it later, when they need it.

> My seventh-grade social-studies teacher would explain our assignment, and then sometimes she would put music on. She made up a song, to remember the order of the presidents. Then she would divide up the class and see what side would know the presidents better, and she would give us the test at the end.   JESSICA

> If we had something wrong in math, my seventh-grade pre-algebra teacher would make us write it down on a piece of paper, and then we would crumple it up. Everyone would have a paper, and we would throw them at each other for three minutes. Then, we would pick up any ball we found and

open it. Whatever that person didn't understand, we would go and try to help them understand it. I didn't know the difference between the angles. This boy told me that an obtuse angle means it's bigger than ninety, and an acute angle means it's less than ninety and a right angle means it's ninety exactly. [It made it easier, because] it wasn't the teacher that you would be nervous in front of, it was a friend.   DENUE

Boys, especially, like games that combine getting the right answer with physical activity or competition. In the descriptions that follow, students clearly connected the games they liked with the different learning goals that their teachers were aiming for. These games can be played in or out of the classroom. (When inside, use soft foam balls!)

Steal the Bacon is a game where you're learning verbs and nouns. There are two teams and there's the "bacon" in the middle, and the teacher will call out a verb, like "run," and the two people that have a verb will have to go and get the bacon in the middle and run back to the other side without getting caught. It's a game of knowing what you learn.   KENSON

Steal the Bacon is not only fun, but actually kids want to get the right answers. Everybody wants to win, so people go and study. You actually feel excited to learn it, instead of like, "Oh, I have to learn this, I don't care."   AMELIA

We played a game for English, and it was about getting to know the stories we were reading better. There were two basketballs in the middle of the court, and two groups. When they call a name, you have to say which story [that character is in], and the person on the other side, they have the same exact question. [As soon as you answer] you go get the basketball, and whoever gets it in the hoop first gets a point.   JAVIER

In seventh grade, we played another game, called Swat. We put vocabulary word cards on the wall, and then two kids at a time get fly swatters. The teacher calls out a definition and we had to hit the word that matched the definition first, with the fly swatter.   KENSON

Sometimes you will want to get kids out of the classroom in order to reignite their interest.

I don't think teachers really like students outside a lot. They should get us out of the classroom more often. My sixth-grade year, when we did weather experiments, my science teacher brought us outside and we got to do different things, like predicting Fahrenheit and Celsius.   KENSON

In sixth grade, we played a game to help us with grammar, like nouns and adjectives. There would be a ball in the middle of the field, and two teams. And when she said "adjectives," we would run and pick the ball up and we would have to use an adjective to describe it, or something else around us in the environment.   DENUE

All kinds of books, websites, and teacher chat groups are filled with other imaginative ways in which teachers can vary instruction. Following are a few that student contributors to this book said they liked:

Teachers shouldn't just say, "Read these things from here to here and answer these questions from this page." One of my teachers did a lot of activities. He made class fun, so I was always looking forward to his class, the way he presented things. Like this one [essay] about the "Nacirema culture"—it's "America" spelled backwards. The whole point was to show not to judge a book by its cover, like judge a culture. GABE

For social studies, we get to do group work to make a scrapbook. We have to go from the West to New York by using different routes. We pick one of the roads and five attractions and do it like a scrapbook. [We have to decide] how to pick the attractions, how to talk about each one—Niagara Falls, Yellowstone Park—and what did you enjoy about that attraction. We got to do a United States map of our routes. We got to do group work, in school and out of school. We picked people in our group that we could just call on the phone and say "Meet me in fifteen minutes at my house, or at the park, or at the library, quickly." We could have one or two days to work it out. DIANA

Right now, we're doing a project [where] they give you a place and people, like the Iroquois, the Maya. Then they tell you to answer the questions, and we're going to the computer to search for pictures and search for answers, and we're going to put it in a poster for each group. You're going to have fun, you're going to be interested, and it's not going to be boring, because you'll be doing something that you like to do. TIFFANY

COMING UP FOR AIR

You can also design activities specifically to help kids regulate their energy level, break the pace, and reestablish desirable levels of focus and energy in the classroom. When you do such an activity, make the point of it clear to students. They will learn that refocusing is an important part of the learning process.

What "Screen Time" Does for Us

Most students in this book take for granted the technology schools provide, particularly computers. When they talk about the role of technology in learning, they focus on video games; overall they regard educational games as inferior to others. Girls and boys have different views, too, on the value of video games in general. A sample of one spirited conversation follows.

On educational video games:

> There's this website called Funbrain, with this game called Math Baseball. You get to pick a math problem like multiplication, division, addition, or subtracting. They'll give you a problem and you'll be batting. If you got the problem right, you'll hit the ball and you'll go to first base, second base. If you answer three problems correctly, you get a home run and you get to play online.   DENUE

> Some computer games could be educational but they're really boring and you don't feel like doing them. There's also computer games that you like to play—football, basketball, soccer—but you're not learning anything, except how to play. But you're not doing anything physical. Why play the game when you could actually be playing it outside? Instead, people are just sitting around.   GENESIS

(continued)

On violence in video games:

I think all video games teach you something, even if it's not what you want to be learning. If you're playing a wrestling game, they teach you how to body slam somebody. If you're playing a violent game, it teaches you how to aim a gun or something, how to hijack a car, kill random people.   DAQUAN

I'm disagreeing with that, because who would want to learn things like that? That can get you into jail.   JESSICA

Most boys have fun playing those games, and some girls, too. If you're smart enough to know that you won't go up on the streets and start shooting cops, then you can play them.   JAVIER

On why we like playing video games:

Middle school students like video games because it might take the stress out of them, after the day. You've done hard work and it could have been a stressful day. It could just calm your mind. I play because they're fun.   DANIEL

When we don't pay attention or we get out of control, some of the teachers try to calm us down by doing other activities, to get us relaxed, or energized, or whatever they want us. The kids don't know it, but it does work.   JESSICA

> My pre-algebra teacher had us get up and do this thing, "5-4-3-2-1 countdown." You did something physical, like "shake your body out" or jumping jacks, as fast as you can five times, and then four and then three and then two and then one.   GABE

You might use a game to change the tempo of the class when kids have too much restless energy.

> One of the things we'd do is "The cold wind blows." There would be one person standing in a circle saying "The cold wind blows." Anybody who's wearing a jacket, they have to hurry up and find a different seat. The person in the middle has to hurry up and sit down, and there's going to be one person left out, and we keep doing that.   JESSICA

> We play "This is a . . ." with two objects that have two syllables, like a marker and a pencil, or a ruler and a pencil. In the circle, you pass the object to the next person and say, "This is a pencil [or whatever it is]." They say, "A what?" and you say, "A pencil." They say, "Oh, a pencil," and then they pass it on and do the same thing. There's two things being passed around, and the whole object of the game is to keep up without losing the beat. If you lose the beat, you're out, and then the circle gets smaller.   GENESIS

Games like this not only motivate middle schoolers and refresh them but also sharpen their learning skills. Kids return to their work more ready and willing to engage.

> A lot of people have trouble keeping their mind on their teacher in class, and that game is an example of keeping your focus on a certain beat, staying on topic and keeping on the beat.   JAVIER

If we wanted to keep on playing games, we would have to calm down afterwards. That's what the teacher would always expect. We always did calm down, because we wanted to play games another day. It's fun now, when he says: "What games should we play?" and everybody's always yelling out different games.   JESSICA

Activities geared toward getting to know each other have an additional value: They create positive feelings across the social subgroups of a middle school classroom.

We get to play, too, in my homeroom. We have Morning Board, and it has an "attendance question"—like "What's your favorite color?" or "What's your favorite animal?"—and when the teacher calls our names to see if we're here, we'll answer the question. We'll have an activity, like "Stoneface." There's a circle with one person in the middle, and that person has to make everybody laugh or smile in less than three minutes.   GENESIS

SETTLING KIDS DOWN

Even when your class is managing well as a group, individual students may be having difficulty maintaining their focus. You will want classroom practices that help them settle down on their own when they get a little itchy. When he reached the middle grades, for example, Gabe often found himself sent out of class for talking, dropping pencils, or other small disruptions. One teacher, however, found a positive way to address his restlessness.

You just step out of the class if you need to and just cool down for a moment and relax, and then come back and do your test or go back to your

work. There was a desk outside, and when I needed to let out my stress I just walked out of the classroom and just sat there for a moment and mellowed out. It wasn't a punishment—you just let the teacher know that you were going. You could take your work out there with you if you needed to.   GABE

Jessica's whole school has adopted a similar practice:

If we get in trouble, we can just walk out of the classroom and go out in the hallway to get our ideas back together. They call it "refocus." The good thing about it is we don't get in trouble for going out in the hallway. It's kind of our choice. The teachers can't go out or try to talk to us. We don't have to tell our parents.   JESSICA

FOOD FOR THOUGHT

The subject of snacks, more than any other, elicited lively debate and commentary from middle school students. Students have strong opinions on the subject of eating or not eating in the classroom, and during the school day. They believe eating more frequently helps them focus in the classroom. Universally, they want to be able to determine when they snack.

They complain about how the kids aren't paying attention in class, and it's because we're not eating. If I don't eat, I get a headache and I lay down on the desk. And then it's, like, "Put your head up." I can't concentrate because I need something in my system.   GENESIS

Kids believe that offering them more opportunities to eat—and to eat enough—will improve their attention and energy for learning.

At my school, we have lunch late. By the time we get to lunch, everybody's hungry. The thing that disturbs most of the kids is the food is real small. I would say the hot dogs are about five inches long. Their hamburgers, the meat is all skinny, so the kids aren't even full. When we go upstairs, the teachers will be, like, "You just had lunch, so pay attention."   DENUE

I think [food] would help you out a lot with your testing. In my elementary school, when we were doing state testing, they gave you a cup of apple juice and some crackers if you were hungry. You could just snack on that and go back to your test.   GABE

Students—especially the girls—also want the choice of eating lunch with their friends.

We do work, then go to lunch, and then we got to sit with the people that we were just in the class with. We should be sitting with our friends.   TATZI

To snack or not to snack? Some schools ban all eating except during lunch. For kids who are rapidly growing, and almost always hungry, this policy proves difficult to enforce.

At my school, you can't eat until lunch. Some kids bring snacks to school and go to the bathroom and eat it when they're hungry, and come back to the class. You're not supposed to do that, but we have last lunch, and if the kid is hungry . . .   JAVIER

Some people used to sneak in class and eat when the teacher wasn't looking.   JESSICA

Other schools have a set time for all students to eat a snack.

> At my school, we get snacks around ten-fifteen, and we get energized for learning better. We buy it from a store and bring it in for our home advisory, which is only sixteen people. At the beginning of the year, the teachers bought it, and now the students buy it.   JESSICA

Many schools leave it up to the teachers to decide, as individuals or as a team of teachers, which can create some confusion for kids.

> We get to eat snacks every day on my team. We bring them from home, and we can eat them anytime in class, as long as we're quiet. But if we get to eat depends on what team we're on. I don't know why they do that, it's weird.   JASON

> In one of my classes, if the kids are really nice, we can bring snacks. But we can only eat it if our teacher's not talking.   JAVIER

Not all students have access to food for snacks, and it often falls to teachers to fill the breach, a nearly impossible task when growing students are always hungry and resources are meager.

> Sometimes in sixth grade, when kids were hungry if we didn't eat breakfast, my teacher would give us a little bar, but she only had so many, so all the class couldn't have it. It was kind of unfair.   KENSON

> When it was hot, at the beginning of the school year, my English teacher brought in two jugs of water for us. She brought in cups and she gave us water when we were thirsty.   KENSON

Let us show you we can eat in class. Students understand there are responsibilities that go along with the privilege of eating in the classroom. If a teacher does have flexibility in establishing eating policies for the classroom, working with students to achieve shared goals can provide a powerful learning experience. Kids want to have the privilege of eating and they are willing to take responsibility for cleaning up.

> The teacher should actually trust us, because in seventh grade, we're not in elementary school. We're not going to make a big mess out of food, and we're not going to try to disturb her by eating. A lot of people can't think right when their stomach is empty.   JAVIER

> In my other school, they wouldn't let us have snacks because it would make a mess to clean up. It's just a little mess, it's not like it's impossible to clean it up—let the kids eat something.   GENESIS

Addressing these issues directly may help students better understand their role in the classroom and in the school—as well as solving the clean-up problems of snacking.

> In my school, they don't let us eat. They say, "Oh, roaches," and that the janitors don't always come and clean up the room like they're supposed to. When I was in seventh grade, they came every day after school, but now, they don't really do it that much.   KENSON

> In my pre-algebra class, when my teacher gives us food, the students have to clean it up. It might only be a little bit, but it makes a big mess, so it takes time out of our period. Fifteen minutes before the bell rings, everybody has to stop what they're doing and clean up their mess. So I'm not crazy about that.   DENUE

Kids understand that the room must be clean and that distractions must be kept to a minimum. They don't want to be unfairly blamed for someone else's mess, and they are therefore ready to agree to rules that ensure individual responsibility.

> Kids should clean up, because it's their mess that they made. Nobody else should be responsible for cleaning up the mess they made. My teacher only makes us clean up the stuff that's under our chairs, because the janitors do a good job cleaning up the room, except they don't go under the desk and chairs. We have two janitors in every floor, so when we get in the classroom in the morning, it's really clean.   DAQUAN

However, they see the teacher as responsible for enforcing these rules of "cleaning up after yourself." They may not be ready to see it as a group responsibility.

> The teacher should stay there and watch the kids when they make the mess. When it's near our desk but we didn't put it there, he shouldn't make us clean it up.   AMELIA

> I think that the teacher should make them clean after every period so he'll know which period made a mess. When most kids eat their sunflower seeds, they spit it all over the floor, and they don't clean it, so if you come into that classroom and you shared that seat, and you have gum or something and you're chewing, the teacher might think that you made all those sunflower seeds all over the floor. Then you have to pick it up.   DENUE

As you work out these matters together, students will begin to understand that you are fair in holding them to higher standards of behavior than they had in elementary school. They will start to see themselves as ready for these standards, and even take pride in meeting them.

SUMMARY
Using Our Energy to Help Us Learn

- Don't ask us to sit still and listen for too long.
- Help us learn what to do when we have too much energy, or too little.
- Vary what we do in class, and we will stay more interested.
- Give us breaks when we are having trouble paying attention.
- Get us thinking, talking, and moving so we will learn better.
- Let us eat more often in school—we're growing! We can learn to clean up after ourselves.

CHAPTER 6

Make Way for Parents

"Parents should change when you get to middle school."

All teachers hope to enlist the parents and guardians of students as supportive partners in their learning. You will have many ways to accomplish this: formal reporting on grades, conferring on student progress, consulting on problem behavior, inviting parents to classroom presentations, and meeting up with them informally at extracurricular events.

Despite your best intentions, however, some of these efforts are likely to backfire. By the time kids reach the middle grades, they are renegotiating their relationship with their parents.

HOW PARENTS CAN HELP

Middle schoolers hope for the help and support of their parents, but they want it in new ways.

Parents should change when you get to middle school. Because when someone starts bugging you in elementary, you just go to your mom, and your mom comes and talks to the teachers and puts that kid in trouble. Nobody cares about who is tough. But when you get in middle school and other kids bother you, your parents should find another way to help you, instead of letting kids think you're un-independent and call you a baby. AMELIA

They need their parents to care about their school experiences.

Parents should care a little more, because a lot of kids are feeling that their parents aren't trying to help them in school. These are the years that school starts getting more important. Middle school actually helps a lot with your future. I think that parents should ask their children about what they did in school, and are they having tough times in school, or is something bothering them in school. Or help them with their homework, stuff like that. JAVIER

But even when they want parental support, middle schoolers are less likely than before to share information with their parents about school.

I think that parents want to be involved. It's just that at this age, we just don't want parents to be in our business. In first or second grade, when my mom asked "What did you do today?" I would go on and on and on. But now that we're in middle school, when they ask us what we did, we go, "School was fine," and that's it. Then we just go to our room. DENUE

Parents often tell teachers that they feel mystified by their own children in the middle grades. They know their children need and want their support, but they no longer know how or when to talk to them. Kids, too, wish their parents could figure this out.

> After school, my dad asks me how my day was. A lot of times, it's not that I even had a bad day at school. I just don't feel like answering—I'm tired or I'm thinking about [how] I have so much work to do. So I'm like, "Ugh"—I just don't answer—and then he keeps doing it. Even if nothing bad has happened, I get really frustrated, like, "Stop asking me how my day was." But when I'm in a better mood, I'm like, "Oh, how was your day, Dad?" Sometimes I think to myself, "Oh, I wish my parents would ask me what I learned today," so I could at least share. But a lot of times if they did do that, I would just be, like, "No, I don't want that." Parents need to know when to back off, when the kid needs space. But they need to know if [there's] something really important to get involved in.   ALMA

The unpredictable moods of students at this age, combined with their desires for more privacy and more freedom, make their seeking support from their parents more challenging for everybody involved.

> Parents don't really get involved like they should, sometimes. Because kids think their parents might be overprotective. You tell your mom there's a school dance. She might say, "I don't want you to go," or, "Yeah, you can go." Sometimes, you might not feel like telling her, because you know how she might react. I don't want my mom to be in my business, but I can't help it. She's just there. If she's going to ask me something, I'm not going to lie, because she wants me to be open with her now that I'm older.   KENSON

> I tell my mom everything, we're really close. My friend, she tells her mom a lot of things, but when it comes to her liking someone, she can't tell her,

because she'll be, like, "No, you can't be liking someone at this age, because I won't let you." GENESIS

Because many students are trying out new social roles and responding to the social forces of school, they may not want their parents to know too much about what is going on.

In school, a lot of the kids don't act the same when their parents [are] around. Some of the kids just act up when the parent isn't around. You see some of the loudest kids in my school get so quiet when the parents come in to meet them. AMELIA

Some imagine they can keep their two worlds of home and school completely separate.

My parents don't usually go to school and they don't need to. 'Cause there's teachers, and that's what teachers are supposed to do. They're supposed to be your parents at school. EDWARD

Others simply feel confused about whether and how they want their parents to support them in school.

Well, yes and no. I want him to be there [at parent conferences], so that he knows what's going on with me and homework and school. And I don't want him to be there, because he might find out some stuff that might be bad, and then he might get mad at me. CANEK

Parents Can Help in Knowing Students Well

It helps a teacher to know, right from the start, what a middle schooler's parents or guardians hope, expect, and believe about their child and school. A number of teachers participating in a MiddleWeb discussion board highly recommend the "million words or less" assignment for parents and guardians, given out on one of the first days of school. The following template might help you create such a letter home.

In a Million Words or Less . . . Tell Me About Your Scholar!

Yes, you are getting a homework assignment! This activity gives you a chance to tell me what you think I should know about your scholar. I will read every letter I receive. I will not share your comments with any other person unless you tell me in your message that I can.

[*Other things to include in your letter home:*]

- Your name, the subject you teach, and your classroom(s).
- Your scholar is in for a great experience in my class this year. We will be studying . . .
- Some highlights of the year include . . .
- You will be able to find important information about our class activities and assignments at . . .

(continued)

- You can contact me in several different ways, including . . .
- Take your time with this assignment, but please return it to me by . . .

You can speak privately to those students in your class whose parents or guardians do not speak or write in English, if you do not understand the language spoken at home. You might ask the student if he or she would be willing to translate or transcribe the parents' "million words or less." Other special situations may also arise; find flexible solutions with students that support school-home communication. In some cases, you may want to ask students to write about the expectations they believe their parents hold for them.

Adapted from teacher suggestions in discussions posted on the website of MiddleWeb: Exploring Middle School Reform (www.middleweb.com).

WHOSE SIDE ARE YOU ON?

Just as parents get mixed messages from their children about the extent to which they should be involved at school, teachers soon learn that their students are desperately hoping they will find the right balance between treating them as newly independent and keeping their families informed.

A thing a lot of teachers make a mistake on, at least in my perspective, is that they call the parents for really little things. In my math class, there was a minor problem that my teacher could have solved right there and then. She called my parents. That makes us feel like we can't trust the teacher, you know? 'Cause some things are really personal. Some things kids don't even want to share with their family. What if it's *about* their family? ALMA

Teachers call home about how kids got in trouble, but sometimes it's not really that big of a deal. I talk a lot in class, so I kind of get in trouble. Or sometimes I get U's for little things, like where maybe you disrupt the class, and a certain amount of U's gets you an "unsatisfactory" warning. Then the teacher ends up calling home, and my mom doesn't believe me, so she ends up getting mad at me. GABE

When teachers get to know what matters to parents, they are often able to work with students more effectively.

My mom takes time to know the teacher. In seventh grade, my history teacher knew my mom, so if I acted up, she would call her. But sometimes, instead of calling when I did something wrong, she would be like, "I know your mom, so I know what you're capable of." Getting to know my mom, she automatically knows some things about me and about my mom—like how my mom would react if I got a bad grade. KENSON

If teachers got to know the parents better, they would know how to deal with kids when they're acting up. Kids go, "Oh yeah, call my parents, I don't care." They get in trouble and they still do it again. But if you got to know their parents and made friends with them, then probably the kids wouldn't act up. AMELIA

Students know you don't have the same time to spend on communicating with parents that their elementary school teachers had.

> In fourth grade, every Friday our teacher would send a letter saying how we did this week, how we behaved this week. We had to sign it on Monday. My mom liked that, because she would be up to date on how I'm being. But sixth, seventh, and eighth, we have more than a hundred students. To be writing a hundred letters every Friday can get teachers mad. DENUE

Still, they want their parents to hear from you about their successes, not just their failures.

> They should send home notes about how you're doing in school, not just notes about how you're acting up. Because I'm good in school, my mom never gets notes at all. I could tell her that I did something good, and says, "Okay, that's nice." But if she has to get a note home, like, "Oh, she did really good today," she'd pay attention to it [more] than me just telling her. GENESIS

Many middle schools use three-way conferences to create partnerships that will facilitate communication between home and school. Students and their parents or guardians meet with the teacher at intervals during the year, to set goals and talk about the student's progress.

More direct contacts with parents, before problems arise, will give you a sense of the level of home support a student has, as well as what the parent or guardian expects from you and from the student. Once you know these things, you have the groundwork laid for periodic communication with your students' families about their growth and progress.

GETTING PARENTS INTO SCHOOL

Although many middle schools communicate with parents by sending general notices home, kids often still look to their teachers to help them keep their families involved in their school lives.

> When there's stuff at school like PTO meetings, we usually get a form and I tell my mom about it, "Mom, this thing is happening at school." She looks at the hours and says, "I can't come, I'm at work." But if she hears it from a teacher, she's more likely to go; "Oh, the teacher's telling me, so I should go." When she hears it from me, it's not that important. GENESIS

You may want to find alternative ways to bring parents into contact with school, which better accommodate their circumstances.

> I think they should send the work home. My mom usually can't come to stuff like PTO meetings. She's always busy, she's always worrying, she's always rushing, she's always got something on her mind. At night, she sits down to drink coffee and I think it would be all right to show her, "This is what I've been doing in school, what I've been learning." When it's at home, she pays more attention to it, and she's proud of me when I get good scores. "That's nice. I guess you understand it good, and you're not having any problems." DENUE

Although students want their parents to understand their academic experiences and appreciate their achievements, parent-teacher communication holds new hazards for middle school students, especially when that communication

Keeping Track of Your Contacts with Parents and Guardians

Knowing more about your students' parents or guardians makes it much easier to communicate with them. You can make copies of this two-page worksheet and use it to make notes as you gather information during the year. *(Note:* Keep this record in a place that will both protect the student's privacy and ensure your easy access.)

Name of student: _____

Name(s) of parent(s) or guardian(s): _____

_____

_____

Best time to reach the parent(s) or guardian(s): _____

_____

Log of My Contacts with the Parent(s)/Guardian(s) of _____

Date of contact	Person(s) contacted	Means of contact (phone, note home, report card, conference, visit, etc.)

Best ways to contact the parent(s) or guardian(s): _____

_____

Is communication with the parent(s) or guardian(s) possible in English? If not, who is available to help? _____

What are the goals and expectations the parent(s) or guardian(s) have for this student?

This year: _____

_____

For the next five years: _____

_____

Note any worries the student has about communications between teacher and parent(s) or guardian(s): _____

_____

Purpose (good news, bad news, required reporting)	Notes on parent/ guardian response	My next steps

occurs at school. Students often feel acutely uncomfortable when their parents show up, even if it is to share their work and success. Sometimes they are concerned about how others will see their parents.

> I don't think they should feel scared, because other parents do it, too. They'll be talking to kids, doing something that embarrasses their kid. I've seen it, tons of times. My parents do it, too.   JASON

If their parents are there to observe their work firsthand, kids also may feel self-conscious and anxious about how their parents see them. But they take special pride in showing parents what they know and can do. Having their parents in school helps bring into balance their worlds of home and school.

> It's harder for me knowing that my mom is there. I had to present a speech, and I thought it was just going to be in front of my class, but it ended up that parents could come. I get nervous, because even though I'm close to her, I feel like I have to impress her more than everybody else there.   GENESIS

> With me, it's hard, I want her there, but then I don't want her there. I do get more nervous, but then I want her to see how good I do. When I had my Spanish project, I got nervous, and then when I didn't see her there, I got upset.   JESSICA

Without the chance to come into school and see for themselves, parents often focus too narrowly on the report card as evidence of how their child is doing. Seeing their child's work in context, along with that of other students, gives parents a more accurate and authentic perspective.

Sometimes I prefer them being there, sometimes I don't, because my dad judges me a lot. I know he's proud of me but he never tells me [that], he only tells me the bad things that I do. When I bring my report card home, if I have all A's and one C, he would go straight to the C and say, "How come you got a C?" So when my dad is there, I want to do really, really good, so he'll actually be proud of me. Sometimes it does me good when my dad is there. But sometimes I feel afraid, "If I do this, then what is my dad going to say, what is my dad going to do?" AMELIA

If You Could Only See

Students in the middle grades often think that their parents do not believe them when they come home with stories about school. Sometimes they wish their parents could witness their school experiences directly.

> There was one time when I wish my dad was there, or my mom, because we have this kind of mean substitute teacher. He shook a kid in our class and so we were really mad at him, and he lied to the principal about [it]. I wish my parents could see what kind of person this teacher actually was. ITAI

Students like Itai realize that when the parents do show up, everybody will be on their best behavior. But their fantasy is that parents could be invisible witnesses to their days.

GRADES, HOMEWORK, AND PARENTS

One of the most difficult things for many students is feeling caught between the world of school, where mistakes are opportunities for learning, and the world of home, where consistent high achievement may be expected.

> On my progress report, I got a C for history, and my mom looked at all the other ones, I had A's on all of them. She didn't even respond to them, she saw the C and she freaked out. I said, "But Mom, look at all the A's I got." JAVIER

Genesis's first science progress report came home showing an unexpectedly low grade.

> My mom was like, "What's this? Why is this happening, you're an A student! Why? Why? Why?" I was trying to explain it to her, and she was like, "Is it your teacher? Because if it's your teacher, I'll go up to the school and I'll talk to him about it." I would say, "No, it's not the teacher. Well, I guess it is the teacher, because he only gave us two homeworks." "Well, you should tell the teacher to give you more homework." I would say, "Ma, I don't want any more homework." And she would say, "But if it would bring that F up, then you should get more homework." GENESIS

Kids are caught in the middle when things like this come up at home. They're afraid their parents will react to bad grades with anger at their teacher.

> [My mom] got mad at me. And then, it was almost the same thing: "Is this teacher being mean to you?" "I don't know." JAVIER

If their parents actually do talk to you about it, kids worry that you will get mad, too.

> If I had a problem because of the teacher, my mom would come to
> the school and start arguing with the teacher, saying, "Why are you
> doing this to my daughter?" and asking a whole bunch of questions.
> I feel embarrassed. After that, the teacher would take all of his angriness
> out on me, like give me bad grades, because my mom came to the
> school. GENESIS

Parents have their ideas of what their child's "doing well in school" looks like. Teachers may have yet another. To complicate things further, kids who do well sometimes face the harsh judgment of their peers. As middle school students learn to navigate these shifting waters, they want their parents to care about their schooling in a way that will provide a steady compass.

> I know so many people, their parents really don't care. I love my mom so
> much because I know how much she suffers. She's always telling me,
> "Don't get into fights, do the best you can in school," and that's what I'm
> always trying to do. You can call me a goody-goody, I don't care, because
> that's how I was raised and I don't mind being like that. It feels good, when
> your parents are proud of something you do at school. She's telling her
> friends that her daughter is a straight-A student, and she's doing things
> that involve academics and stuff.   GENESIS

> [When my mom saw my report card] she said, "You could do better." And
> then, I thought I could do better. That helps me, to know that I could do
> better in school, so then my mom won't get mad at me.   JAVIER

Homework often provides a useful arena in which parents can demonstrate their fundamental support for students' academic efforts.

> My father's the homework patrol. Whenever I do my homework, or whenever I come home from school, I wish he wasn't there. 'Cause he's going to start asking me what homework I have, and he's going to start looking over my shoulder and making sure that it's getting done correctly. It gets annoying. Maybe he's being concerned a little too much, coming over and checking on me every ten minutes. But there are times when I do want him there, when I need a boost—like in a speech or a performance, where I might want my parents or my father to be there. CANEK

But there will be students whose parents, for any number of reasons, do not provide that support for students to get their homework done at home.

> Another reason why kids act up is because they're under pressure at home. Where I live, there's a lot of kids who are out of school, like fourteen-year-olds and nine-year-olds. You hear them on the streets swearing. My next-door neighbor, her son would come home from school, and I would help him do his homework. All she has to do after is sign the paper, and it would take her days before she signs. It's not like she doesn't care about him. She would say, "Oh, if you go out there and start trouble, don't come to me crying." But it's like she doesn't really care about his education, about what he learns at school. If he goes to school and starts acting up, I don't think it's his fault. I think it's his mom's fault. AMELIA

COMMUNITY AND AFTER-SCHOOL PROGRAMS

The programs many students attend after school or in the community also give them a place to integrate the competing pulls they experience from different quarters. Such programs may focus on homework or tutoring, on the arts, or on physical activities—whatever their focus, at their best, they create a safe place in which young adolescents can ground their ever-changing selves.

> You gotta find something to preoccupy your time. Just get into a program, like a drama club or [an after-school program]. All schools have them. Once you get there, they got tutors that will help you, so you won't have to study by yourself. BRIAN

After-school sports provide a way for many students to bring together their family and school experiences.

> My dad, he's been trying and trying to get me on to a soccer team, but no one had a spot open. So now that my school has a soccer team, I'll be able to play. I want to be in the tradition of my family—I really like playing soccer, even though we lose a lot. When I know there's a soccer game or a practice, I feel more enthusiastic to go to school. GENESIS

For Tiffany and Diana, a youth leadership program in their New York neighborhood gives them a chance to express and connect different parts of themselves.

> I get to talk. I get new activities, not the same thing every day. We go to a group and we do all the work that [the adult leader] has given us. Then we make a circle to present our youth newsletters and things like that. It makes me feel good. At school, I do work, but it's just work. Here, I get to express

myself and I get to do different things. The other day, we were doing projects, we were saving up money for Hurricane Katrina. In school, I'm helping myself. Here I'm helping other people who need help, which is important.   TIFFANY

In my school, you don't do that much activities. You have to do homework. You have to pay attention to the work that they're giving you at that point. For math, you have to talk about related things about that subject. You can't talk about what you did on the weekend, or what you're planning to do. When you go to this community program, we can talk about what we want to talk about. You don't have to bring a book bag, you don't have to take notes. You just have to bring an open mind here, tell about your feelings. You do different activities—newsletters, sending people information about our youth leader program.   DIANA

Genesis learned how to be a peer mediator in an after-school program.

The instructor would tell us about how peer mediators are not supposed to tell people, "You have to apologize." You get the two people, ask them questions, hear each person's side of the story. Let them figure out possible solutions, let them see if they want different solutions, if the solutions fit right and let them apologize if they want to. They don't have to apologize right there and then. [Now] in school, I'm really good at solving problems—people are in fights and I help them solve it. I just like doing it. I like helping.   GENESIS

As you look for ways to bring parents into the school and school into the home and community, you may be pushing against many tides—parent-child dynamics, student-student forces, limited community resources, the demands on your own time as a teacher. But even making modest headway will help students begin to weave together the emerging roles they are trying out at school, at home, and in the neighborhood. With sufficient support, they will integrate those roles into a sense of self that includes being a good student. If all goes well, they will move into high school with the desire to succeed.

SUMMARY
Make Way for Parents

- We want our parents' help and support, but we want it in new ways.
- We don't want to share everything about school with our parents.
- We want our parents to see and take pride in our accomplishments.
- We need our parents to help when we have a problem in school.
- We want you to balance our need to feel more grown up with your responsibility to keep our parents informed.
- We need you to get to know our parents and what matters to them.

CHAPTER 7

Our Transition to High School

"That's all I was thinking about all summer long, staying up late: what's high school going to be like?"

By the time students hit eighth grade, the transition to ninth grade looms large. Their middle school teachers are talking more urgently about the need to prepare for high school standards, both in behavior and in academics. Friends and siblings already in high school are warning them that everything is about to change, big time. They worry about their social world turning upside down, as they move from the top to the bottom of the grade-level pecking order. Depending on the way their school system works, they might have to enter their new world without the safe feeling of having friends in it with them.

Young teenagers realize that ninth grade marks the beginning of a new, high-stakes period of their lives. Out in the real world, people tell them, it will really matter how they behave and whether they succeed in high school.

When you get to ninth grade, there's no more playing. It's all about serious business. You got to get about your work. You gotta find a study habit. You gotta do the right thing. Because after ninth grade, that determines where you're gonna be in life. How you gonna get paid, and how you gonna get treated—upper class, lower class. High school is going to follow you throughout your whole life. BRIAN

In middle school, it really isn't that important to you, you just coming to school and getting the basics. But high school gets you ready for getting a job. They gonna look at your high school scores, not your middle school scores, or how you was doing in first grade. If they see that you were playing throughout the whole high school years they might think, "This person is going to play on the job." GEOFFERY

In the social world of high school, kids hear, the stakes are equally high. Even though they are eager to get on with the experience, they also wonder now—just as they wondered entering middle school—if they will be able to handle its new demands.

I think it's going to be tough to fit in with people that I don't know. They might get the wrong impression about me, and I might have trouble. KENSON

WHAT IS THERE TO WORRY ABOUT?

When they are imagining themselves in high school, kids draw on a vast store-house of lore passed on from students who have gone before them. Fed by the rumor mill (and sometimes also by teachers' warnings), their worries echo those they had a few years before, but on a grander scale.

High school will be huge and confusing. Much larger than the typical middle school, the average United States high school enrolls over a thousand students, and sometimes many times more. Unless they are headed for a small high school, kids imagine an overwhelming scene. In a crowded school short on human and financial resources, the prospect grows even more scary.

> All my buddies told me that high school was going to be a zoo, people running around, nobody going to class. Up on every corner, people just standing there like light posts, with no worry about getting an education. It's so big here, there's like two thousand kids. I'm thinking, "How they gonna manage it?"   BRIAN

> You have to get used to carrying around seven or eight textbooks. Your locker is in a different building than half of your classes, and that's really hard.   RACHELL

They fear that they will get lost in a large building or campus, and that others will make them look foolish and ignorant.

> They say not to ever ask anybody older for directions because they'll always say, "Oh yeah, your classroom's right there," and you'll end up being on the other side of the campus.   HEATHER

The class schedule will be too complicated. Many middle schools, though not all, have students move from class to class with different teachers. But high school schedules include more electives and often more class periods. When kids picture negotiating that in a large physical setting and with skimpy "passing time" between classes, they start to worry.

The only time we changed classes in [my K–8] school was going to either P.E. [physical education], music, or art. So I was nervous about coming into high school, getting used to going from one class to another.   CHANTÉ

The homework load will overwhelm us. With more classes and more at stake in each of them, students know that high school will probably make new demands on them. They worry about losing their freedom to hang out and have fun with friends.

My friend who's in high school, he told me that they give him a lot of homework, and sometimes I don't like to do homework.   KENSON

They expect you to do six hours of homework in a night, 'cause each class will give you an hour worth of homework. But I'm on the phone three hours after I get home, talking to my friends.   RACHELL

Older students will haze and bully us. Exaggerated or not, stories take hold everywhere of how students in upper high school grades pick on and humiliate the new ninth graders. Even the most confident newcomers know they will need ways through the ritual of humiliation. Kids who feel shy, physically underdeveloped or overdeveloped, or otherwise vulnerable, worry even more.

In eighth grade, my friends and I all thought we were the big shots of the school. Then you come here and you're taken down three notches. You're at the bottom of the food chain. Even if you're a "popular" ninth grader, there are still seniors who will take you down. They'll be, "Go away, you little freshman."   RACHELL

[My friends in high school] be telling us that we're going to be fresh meat, that they're going to be torturing us and stuff. Like if we run our mouth to either juniors or seniors, they would jump you.   CHANTÉ

My brother said that they have a certain day that they throw the freshmen and some sophomores in trash cans, throw people in the creek, lock them out of their classrooms, hit them, pick on them.   ASHLEY

WHEN REALITY SETS IN

It doesn't take long, however, for new ninth graders to figure out which of their fears will come to pass and which will probably not. Only a few weeks after the start of high school, they describe their transition in more realistic terms—some positive, some less so.

High school gives you a fresh start. Not everyone knows their past when they arrive in ninth grade, so students sometimes take advantage of the chance to change their image, either academically or socially. Hoping to avoid humiliation in the new school setting, they may focus on their work habits or cultivate new friends.

Once you get to ninth grade, you don't want everybody to think that you're a goofy or silly person. So you try to become more mature so everybody will give you more respect. They do give you a second chance. Last year I wasn't that good in school, but right now, I'm doing pretty good.   GEOFFERY

I had a very dramatic middle school year. I been in trouble, I went through depression, I got into a relationship with someone who misled me. This year, I feel like new, 'cause there's a whole bunch of new people, plus my best friend goes here.   HEATHER

The support of a good friend does matter enormously to new ninth graders. Without it, a student's "fresh start" may mean retreating into a protective solitude to ward off new hurts.

During the summer after eighth grade, all my friends ditched me and turned their backs on me. When I got to ninth grade, I was scared and didn't talk to no one. I just want to keep to myself more, 'cause I didn't want nothing like that to happen again.   BRANDON

Guarding against social stigma also involves careful calculations about personal appearance. As in middle school, high school students still sort themselves according to clothing styles and body decoration.

I see that a lot of people are cliqued off—maybe not purposely, but just by the way everybody's dressed. People who call themselves alternative, they're all with the purple hair and the what-not. Or ghetto, where your shoes cost more than, like, the rent. Then there's the people who keep to themselves: they're really smart and they do their work and they don't really socialize with anybody else.   HEATHER

But ninth graders also notice that their high school peers cross those subgroups more than the middle school scene permitted.

In eighth grade, you had to fit in or you were like a nobody. In ninth grade, your personality and characteristics, they're the same, but your image can be totally different. You can just dress how you want to and still have friends.   ASHLEY

Back in middle school, everybody wanted to be like everybody else. If you weren't like that, then you got picked on. But now, you can do your own thing and everybody's your friend. A lot of my friends in the beginning of this year were scary Goth punk people, and I liked the scary black stuff, back then. But now, I'm a preppy person.   RACHELL

High school work starts where middle school left off. Students go into ninth grade with anxiety that the academic work will be much harder than before. When their new teachers instead build new material on their prior knowledge and skills, students regain confidence that they can do well.

They go step by step, they don't teach you stuff that you don't know. They just review, then take you to the next step. So then it's not that hard.   ALEX

I thought that with getting us ready for all the tests, we were going to have a hard time with math and language arts. But first they just review what you learned last year. Then they might add something that will help make it easier, like they might show you an easier method of doing fractions than what you learned last year.   GEOFFERY

High school teachers have less time for individual students. If they are responsible for the typical high school load of over 120 students, teachers usually have little time to give ninth graders the individual attention they may have received in middle school. This can come as a rude shock, especially to students who struggle to keep up.

Some of the work was hard, and the teachers have you do notes off the overhead all the time. I couldn't keep up with it, 'cause I'm a slow writer.   BRIAN

There's so many of us, it's hard for the teachers to get to know you. So kids expect that they're gonna get special help, like they did in middle school. But if you're really quiet, then teachers, they don't care. We jumped from these really nice teachers to these bitter ones who don't want to help you.   HEATHER

The classes are forty minutes, and they go by really fast. It doesn't seem like I'm getting enough of one thing—it's just jumping around, and it's too hard. They give me a lot of homework—too much for that little class time, I think.   KAITLYN

Teachers cut you less slack if you mess up. The workload escalates in ninth grade, so it's easy for students to fall behind. They may not expect the matter-of-fact consequences a busy high school teacher can deal out.

Before, I could do one homework paper a night and still get an A in that class. In ninth grade, there are more classes, and each class gives you double what you got in middle school. I can't get it all done.   RACHELL

In middle school, the teachers were, like, "Maybe I can help you out a little bit." Here, they're just, like, "Well, get out then. Who cares?" It's a good thing, 'cause that wakes people up that in high school you can't have things done for you, you have to do it for yourself.   HEATHER

Consequences for misbehavior, as well, often come in more impersonal form than what students have experienced in middle school. Especially at a large high school organized in conventional ways, they may be on their way to detention or worse, with no questions asked.

In middle school, it was a lot more socializing. As long as you did their work, the teachers didn't care if you was late or if you stood in the halls and talked. Now they're a little more strict.   ASHLEY

There's just a couple people that are still trying to keep it down. Half of them I know, and they're already realizing that school ain't a joke. It's not tolerated. You get a couple chances, then you're expelled. After that, that's when dropout comes.   BRIAN

You have to balance schoolwork with social life. As teachers are expecting more from students, ninth graders are also getting better at managing the social distractions that pull them away from academics.

I thought that I wouldn't survive high school, 'cause all you do is do work and study. I thought maybe I wouldn't even go to class, I'd drop out. But now it don't seem that hard, because studying is a major part of school. When you start studying, you ain't got to worry about going out in the streets and getting into all types of stuff.   NYESHA

A lot of boys here pay attention to me and like to socialize with me. Now I'm more mature, and I understand that I can socialize and do my work at the same time. As long as I can keep my grades up I can do whatever.   ASHLEY

As they try out new work and new ways, ninth graders gradually begin to develop a new perspective on their former selves.

When I was in middle school, I felt like I was big. Kids, they felt like they gotta put on a front, try to do what the crowd do, be popular and cool.

That's *all* middle school is about. It was gossiping everywhere. A fight could just happen on the sixth-grade floor and you would hear about it in the eighth-grade hall like *that*.

Now that I'm in ninth grade and I look at all the sixth, seventh, and eighth graders, I'm, like, "Dang, was I that little?" High school ain't about coming to look the fly-est. Once you get to ninth grade, it's just, "Quit being childish, and be yourself." Everybody's starting to understand and get a better perspective. You have to strive to do your work, pass your class, graduate, go to college, marry a girl who's going to be something, have kids later on . . . live.   BRIAN

HOW TO HELP BEFORE NINTH GRADE

Teachers in the middle grades can do a lot to help students manage their worries and prepare for the big transition to high school. Looking back after the first month in their large urban high schools, ninth-grade students offered the following suggestions.

Connect us up with high school students. Teachers can talk about ninth grade all they want, but kids prefer to hear it straight from the source.

I don't think that middle school students particularly listen to teachers' advice anyways, but maybe they'd listen to high schoolers better, and feel better about what to expect at high school. Once I got into sixth or seventh grade, they had us write letters to fifth-grade students about what to expect. So maybe high school students could write letters to middle school students.   HEATHER

Seventh and eighth graders want to meet ahead of time with students who are already succeeding in high school. From their vantage point as new ninth graders, students like Geoffery and Ashley, below, say they also want to share their experiences.

> They could have a child follow one high school student for a day, so they have a better idea of how their day is.   GEOFFERY

> We could pick a middle-school class to go back and visit, like with one of our favorite teachers. I would ask the teacher what she tells them, then I would tell them the real truth about what high school is like—that it's really nothing to be worried about, you just need to work hard and be yourself.   ASHLEY

The personal connections eighth graders start to make with older students can ease their fears about the hard transition period. Even one person at the new school who can reach out a friendly hand makes a huge difference.

> The high schoolers can come talk to the kids about how it feels to be in high school. What changes they have to go through, who they have to go through it with. And where they will be going—if the campus is big, they can bring maps, they can take them to the school and give tours.   NYESHA

> One of my family's a sophomore right now. Me and him started talking and I started meeting more of his friends, so we started becoming buddies.   JOSÉ

Support us in developing skills and strategies for high school success. In seventh and eighth grade, kids need lots of practice and reflective talk about what they will need to succeed in high school. Teachers can start by giving them the chance to tackle new responsibilities—facilitating a class group, organizing an event, mentoring younger students, mediating conflicts. At the same time, adults should provide the support that students need in order to do well at their new tasks.

> Going into thirteen years old, we're starting to turn into adults, so we're not really sure what's expected of us. Maybe the schools could realize that and help us to understand that better. They can make the place more mature. Make middle school as close to high school [as they can], so that it won't be that big of a change. We wouldn't be that much different from the bigger students. GEOFFERY

Academic support programs especially designed for middle grades students can help them start to develop attitudes and habits they will rely on later, when they face the challenges of high school.

> Most students just think, "Oh my God—numbers, words, reading . . ." But really school ain't about that. It's about learning strategies. Everything is like a formula, and once you learn the formulas you can't forget them. You just keep doing it over and over, you don't have to think. It becomes something that you know. BRIAN

Girls may feel different pressures in middle school than boys do, and they appreciate the chance to explore these new challenges together.

> Our school established the Pink Ladies, just for girls in seventh and eighth, where every Tuesday and Thursday you meet with a different speaker telling you about the different things that you can experience in your personal life.

We also talked about what you can and cannot do to move forward in your life.   NYESHA

Help us make strong and mutually respectful connections with adults. For better or worse, students count their relationships with middle school teachers as among their most important. When teachers respond with empathy and respect to their efforts, struggles, and worries, it can have a big effect on their attitudes and behavior as they move on to high school.

> Eighth-grade teachers try to scare students about high school, and then we come in really nervous. I don't think they should say, "Oh, it's nothing." They should tell us, "You're going to have a lot more work to do, and it's probably going to be a little harder." Not to be afraid, but not to be careless, either.   HEATHER

Situations in which young people and adults together do things that matter to all involved (service projects, school publications or events, discussion groups on important issues) create a context in which mutual respect grows. They also give kids the chance to try on more mature roles.

> When kids hang around kids, without adult supervision, they're going to act immature. But they got all these programs about "go in there and talk," where kids come to sit down with a whole lot of thoughts and all-level older people. If you got the right adult there showing them the right way to be more mature, who's going to act childish?   BRIAN

Middle schoolers also gain confidence when their teachers and mentors treat them as people who can achieve a bright future, passing on the nonacademic skills they will need to handle life in the adult world.

Starting in eighth grade, we used to have special guests come in to talk to us about how it's really going to be when you go to try to get a job—things that they say, how to greet them, shake their hand. How when you're talking to them, you don't come with no yes-or-no question, you come with something that you all can talk it out.   BRIAN

Provide "bridge" experiences in the summer after eighth grade. New ninth graders have a big advantage if they can start high school with some of their pressing worries put to rest. Being able to find their way around the campus, recognizing some familiar faces in the crowd, getting a jump start in the academic arena—all these can ease the anxiety of the newcomer and make a successful transition more likely.

Training for an athletic team in the summer before high school offers many students this advantage. Going to practices allows the younger students to get to know older students in an atmosphere of structure, discipline, and high expectations. Well before eighth graders graduate, middle schools can do them a favor by helping match up their sports interests (as well as other interests like music or drama) with opportunities at the high school they will attend.

I expected to try out for volleyball when the year started, but my friend who has a sister in volleyball said, "Oh, you start right at the beginning of the summer." How are freshmen supposed to figure that out?   HEATHER

In football practice, you get to know the upperclassmen better, before they put a label on you to say they don't like you or anything. You get to talk to 'em, get to know their personality and everything.   CHRISTOPHER

Summer school can offer another bridge to high school, if it is not presented as punishment for failure but as a chance to get a head start and make friends. Summer study becomes even more of an advantage if the program takes place on the high school campus.

> It wasn't required, you could do it if you wanted to, and I wanted to get used to the campus before I got here. We got to know a lot of people, because it was freshmen and sophomores and juniors and seniors together. Simple things—I just don't have to worry, because the majority of everybody, I had met them. Some people I still don't know, but they come up to me like I know them.   NYESHA

Kids also may find that summer school equips them with academic grounding and reinforcement, once the school doors open in the fall.

> We had two different teachers, one for math, the other for English. Some of the stuff we was doing, we have not seen yet; they was teaching us stuff that was above us. But it was getting us ready for it, before it comes. They was basically treating you like you was in high school. Then, when it comes, it's easier for us.   NYESHA

HOW TO HELP IN THE NINTH-GRADE YEAR

High schools can also take steps that help new ninth graders through the transition and build a solid foundation for their success. Even after only a month in their new high schools, students had this advice about what worked best for them:

Create smaller learning communities for us. New high school students are more likely to find their academic and social bearings if their learning community feels small enough that they can be known well by others. Most safe and welcoming is a community of no more than a few hundred students, guided by teachers who work in collaborative teams.

> In elementary and middle, you interact more with the teachers, and they know you more. They take it out of their own time to try to talk to the children over and over. But at high school you only see the teacher forty minutes a day. By the time our year came for ninth grade [the 2,000-student high school] had already broken up into small schools. That helped. Things been going all right for me. BRIAN

Group ninth graders together in one physical setting. Ninth graders in schools with a large building or campus (with more than a few hundred students) report that if they occupy the same physical spaces, they find it easier to get to classrooms. Their proximity with their new classmates also encourages social bonding and support.

> You could just wander on for hours here, trying to find the right building. You could end up in the wrong classroom, with everybody laughing at you—that's really embarrassing. HEATHER

> I was nervous, but I got over it, after about a week, when I realized I had friends in all my classes. I only got lost my first day here, 'cause all my classes are really close together. AMANDA S.

Start our year with a ninth-grade orientation period. Coming into an unfamiliar high school, first-year students appreciate extra time to sort out their schedules, find their way around, get to know teachers and fellow students, and ask questions without fearing ridicule.

> It was kinda cool 'cause the first week didn't seem real. We was in big groups, just to help you and support you. Every FA [Faculty Adviser] teacher gave each person a map of the school, just getting to know the buildings and how to get there. They showed you your schedule, then they showed you the times that you go from class to class.   NYESHA

> One thing that was nice was that teachers and cops around would tell you, "Go this way." Instead of asking people you didn't know, you could ask the teachers standing around. They did that for a week.   KAITLYN

> You have all those older students to tell you, "When you do this, that's not going to work out good for you in the long run." So then you have a model as to what not to do.   GEOFFERY

Match us up with student mentors. Some high schools have a buddy system that pairs new ninth graders with a tenth or eleventh grader, to establish a bond with a student who recently managed the same transition. Mentors go through a training period, then check in with their ninth-grade buddies regularly all year. Particularly in the first weeks of school, it provides a welcome safety net.

> I met my mentor the first day of school; he was one of the first people that I talked to. First we meet in a group and then we go one-on-one with them from there. They help you out, they take you different places, they introduce you to different things you've never seen. He's like a big brother to me, a good friend. He's there for me when I need him.   CHRISTOPHER

We get together every Tuesday after school, from two-thirty till four. We'll break down into groups with our mentors and then we'll have a one-on-one conversation. Sometimes we'll have a snack. You can tell in the way they look at you and talk to you that they're a nice person. I figured that if she was nice, then everybody would be nice.   CHANDYN

As the year goes on, ninth graders are also encouraged to go to their student mentors for academic help, or to sort out difficulties with teachers or peers.

If you're doing homework and you don't know what you're doing, there's someone by your side. Even class work—if you don't understand something, you can get a pass from your teacher and go to your mentor, talk to them about it and they can help you out.   CHANDYN

If a person's picking on you or if a teacher's not being fair with you, they probably going to listen to him better than you, 'cause he's older. He can go to them and talk it out, and probably solve the problem better than what we could.   CHRISTOPHER

Build advisory groups into our schedule. Belonging to a group of about fifteen that meets regularly with a faculty adviser helps students better manage the high school transition. Whether the group consists only of ninth graders or mixes in students from upper classes, it can offer a haven in which to build relationships and get academic guidance and support.

We take five minutes out of every period on Wednesdays, to make advisory period for fifty minutes. Its whole purpose is to help you and to talk about what they can do to better the school. My advisory teacher, he knows me very well. He helps us out with any problems and, if we have any homework or anything that we need to make up, we can do it in that class.   CHRISTOPHER

The advisory periods make it a whole lot easier. My adviser is one of my teachers, and we're like real cool. We just clicked automatically. I can go to her and tell her anything and she won't say nothing. Sometimes at the end of the period they ask if anybody needs homework help, or class help, or directions to any class.   ASHLEY

I like the advisory class 'cause it gives you a little extra time that you need to study. You don't get a credit for the class, but once you think about it, it's to help you get all your credits for the other classes.   BRIAN

If we got something on our chest, we can talk to that teacher. We can associate among the students that have that adviser.   CHANDYN

Design classroom activities to connect with us personally. To new ninth graders, high school classes can seem intimidating at first. It helps if the teacher starts the year by showing interest in getting to know students, and helping them get to know each other.

Teachers can make it easier for us by [giving us] more get-along activities. Working in groups, and asking your group where'd they come from, where'd their name come from, what we like to do, what school we came from, stuff like that. We did that in my literature class, and in that class I can actually talk to more people more than any other class, 'cause I know more people.   BRANDON

Keep the class focused on learning. Sometime around the transition period into high school, many adolescents gain a growing sense of seriousness about themselves as students.

> Sometimes people in my class are talking and passing notes and it's kind of destructive when I'm trying to work. That's basically making the whole class slow down, 'cause the whole class is dependent on the slower kids. So how they're going, that's the speed of how we're going.   ITAI

They become less tolerant of distractions from their less purposeful classmates, and they want their teachers to hold everybody to norms that support learning.

> Teachers might give you a little bit of leeway, knowing that you just came out of middle school, but also they want you to get in gear for the rest of the year. If you're playing games or hiding people's stuff, they'll say, "That's middle school behavior. I'm not babysitting kids." In high school you're getting ready for being an adult, and as an adult you wouldn't do childish things like that.   GEOFFERY

> You only got forty minutes of class. If the teacher spends a whole class period trying to put a child in his place and in line—now, who's going to learn something?   BRIAN

> One or two people in a class just have to be the class clown and have to go to the dean's office two or three times a day. If teachers have to mess with them for the first week, you don't get to know your teachers. If they don't care about their learning, fine, but just don't interrupt everybody else's.   RACHELL

Give us extra help, both in and out of class. Experiencing some academic successes early on in ninth grade can help set an important pattern of accomplishment and pride. Offering individual support is especially important, both with class work and homework, so that ninth graders do not fall behind and get discouraged.

> You can't miss not one day of class, and then once you get home from school, you got to study about what you did in class. 'Cause we only got like forty minutes, per class, so it ain't enough time—especially in math. BRIAN

If an extra teacher or aide can be assigned to help out in the classroom, all the better.

> In my biology class, because we have two teachers in the room, there's enough time for everybody to ask their questions and get the help they need. It's a lot easier, and I'm passing that class with a B. AMANDA S.

Another approach builds time into the school schedule for supported study groups or tutoring.

> I can't get much studying in, 'cause I'm a football player, and I come home sore and everything. So I have to have my fifth period just to study. A lot of people in there. JOSÉ

Some students will have family responsibilities that interfere with their adjustment to high school and will need extra support in school. They might be caring for older relatives or younger siblings, or they might even have children of their own.

> The first week of ninth grade I missed 'cause I had a daughter being born. I had to do all my makeup work, pull up my grades. All my grades were down, I had like three F's.   BRANDON

After-school homework groups also help, especially when someone is there to supervise and answer questions if students are stuck. Sports teams sometimes require such study groups, with players making success a team priority.

> On the football team, we have study table every night on Tuesday, Wednesday, and Thursday, and the older kids can help you out with your homework if you need it. That's another good experience.   CHRISTOPHER

Extra activities help kids succeed at things they care about. When new ninth graders have the chance to take part in activities outside of class, they gain new reasons to care about coming to school. As they work on things they care about with other students and adults, their identity as part of the school community grows stronger and more important to them.

> Two upperclassmen I know that are on the football team help downstairs in the cafeteria, selling candy and stuff. That's a good experience for us, to imprint on what they're doing right now. So that when we get into the upper classes, we'll be able to help the school as well as they did.   CHANDYN

HIGH SCHOOL IS DIFFERENT

By four weeks into their ninth-grade year, students already have a good sense that they are in a whole new world, with a new hierarchy of people and priorities. They may step up to the plate with interest and excitement, but at times they miss the younger selves they have now left behind.

> I definitely think little twelve-year-olds are too immature to come to high school. The main message that I could give to an eighth-grade student is, "Be prepared, just not too prepared." And don't try to grow up too fast, 'cause once you start hitting your teen years sometimes you wish you were just little again.   HEATHER

SUMMARY
Our Transition to High School

- Provide time for us to ask lots of questions about how things are going to change in high school.
- Arrange for us to hear from high school students before we get there.
- Let us visit our new school to experience a typical day there.
- Give us practice in the skills we will need in high school.
- Provide "bridge" experiences in the summer after eighth grade.
- Tell our ninth-grade teachers what helps us do well in school.
- Connect us up with mentors or buddies in the high school.
- As you send us off to high school, let us know you believe we are ready.

Epilogue: Through the Kaleidoscope

"Teachers don't know what the kids are thinking; they only make a guess."

I f you have already spent time teaching in a middle-grades classroom, you know that good advice from experts can only get you so far. To survive and even enjoy that experience, you have to hold up to your mind's eye the kaleido-scope of early adolescence. The images inside—bright, diverse shapes falling into new patterns at every turn—never stay still for long. Shifts in time and space change the picture, and so does the choice of which end of the kaleido-scope to look into. Yet this moment's view is not right and the next moment's wrong. Each scene has its interest and value; each can change with even the smallest nudge.

This book hopes to help you use those kaleidoscopic images to grow in your teacherly skills, wisdom, and humor. The middle-grades teachers that we ad-mire most gained their seasoned perspectives after years of looking at such con-tinual shifts. They now both understand and expect the daily surprises that middle school students spring on teachers. These veteran teachers gradually changed the way they looked at things, and as a result, they now look at things they might once have never noticed. Just as important, the things they see in their classrooms look different to them. Even a fire in the bathroom can tell them something, once they are willing to ask what's behind it.

Such professional development cannot be handed over as a tidy notebook filled with lesson plans. Instead, growth will come with your close observation of students over the years, your tries at opening up communication with them. We hope that the student voices in this book will help you develop those skills, so that you notice in a new way what your own students say and do.

You will find, as we did here, that the statements and behavior of early adolescents do not organize into neat categories or simple prescriptions. Even though you try for consistency in your interactions with students, a list of rules cannot help you deal with their contradictions. When confronted with your own failures or theirs, you might blame yourself, or you might blame the kids. But either way, you would be missing the point, as Jessica, a seventh grader, points out:

> Teachers don't know what the kids are thinking, they only make a guess.
> And their guesses aren't even right, or next to right.

You don't need to be paralyzed however, when everything you thought you knew collapses into another picture altogether. Instead, as you go in to school each day, you can simply meet your students where they are. You may feel overwhelmed by a sense that you have to somehow manage, negotiate, and get right all the shifting factors in your classroom. That's not possible—but having a sense of humor *is* possible.

As you experiment with the "best practices" that so many books set out, pay attention to how each of those recommendations works, and doesn't work, with your kids. See what you can learn by listening closely to what students tell you. Gradually, you will discover ways to shape your own best practice.

You may have decided, for example, to use a game to enliven the classroom—but the students won't play. That doesn't mean that you should never try a game again. Instead, explore with the class why the game was a flop. What were their social concerns? Did the game seem too silly or childish? Did they see no connection to serious learning? Did they understand the rules? Did they just come in from P.E.?

Or you may have given a really interesting homework assignment, and then more than half the class doesn't do it. How many of the students do not have a long enough period of undisrupted time at home to do it? How many, once they left the context of the classroom, no longer understood what you wanted them to do? What skills were embedded within the project that they had not yet mastered? Who else gave them homework to do that night? As you learn the answers, you will find ways to help them better meet their academic responsibilities.

If you start with the student's point of view in mind, the things you see will change, as master teachers have discovered. The secret is to keep your focus squarely on the learning goals, while being willing to radically adjust your strategies to fit what's really going on with students. Then, if your lively game flops in the first five minutes, you won't need to panic. You won't expect the path to your learning goal to be straight or uncluttered by the real people on it. You'll see where you're going, and you will get there together.

Early in this book, we asked you to think back on your own experiences in the middle grades. Many of the teachers who complete this exercise remember the confusion, doubt, and even pain they felt in school at that age. Yet they often find it difficult to see how those experiences influence their responses to the young adolescents in their classrooms. Unearthing those memories can help you understand why you enjoy some students more than others, and why some kids seem to push your buttons more. This happens because we ourselves, in early adolescence, were buffeted and shaped by the same dynamics you see in your classroom. We can still hear those echoes today, if we listen for them. And as we understand where they come from, we can gradually bring more students into our "sympathy zone."

Middle school kids today are growing up in a dramatically different social context than their teachers experienced, because of changes in our world and our communities. They encounter greater dangers in their lives, and so, more than ever, they need safe classrooms in which to communicate, try new things, and grow up. But the developmental process remains the same as when we were their age, and so does the role of the teacher. Just as we did then, kids today want to learn, to love, to be accepted, and to be really good at something. They do not want to fail, and they do not want to feel ashamed.

We all made it through the middle grades somehow, and you have returned as a teacher. Looking back, you might remember someone at school whose attention and interest made a difference in your own early adolescent years. Now, you have the chance to offer that same attentive ear, understanding, respect, and guidance. Doing so will not detract from your important role as an academic coach. In fact, it greatly strengthens your ability to teach students effectively.

As everyday challenges arise in your classroom, we hope this book helps you loosen your clutch on the list of tactics you bring into the classroom. Instead, we hope, you will begin to relax and recognize the places where you and the students can meet.

As one veteran middle-grades teacher told us, "Sometimes, they have to move because you expect them to be a certain way. And sometimes, *you* have to move in order to accommodate their needs and help them learn." As you begin to understand the developmental journey of young adolescents, she continued, "You will find the right time to say, 'Yes, I understand—but *you* still need to . . .' and the right time to say, 'Yes, I understand, *therefore I need to . . .*' "

Middle school students know that their actions often bewilder their teachers, who are left guessing about what they want and why they want it. But kids are willing to talk about it, if we are willing to listen as they reveal the various layers of their complex reality. With time, we think you will agree with Kenson, an eighth grader, who explained why he wanted his words in this book:

> Our suggestions can help teachers figure out how kids really act, and how they learn, and can help teachers think about what kids do.

What Are Your Students Ready For?
An Exercise for Teachers

With middle-grades classes, it can sometimes be hard for a teacher to know what kinds of challenges the students are ready for, and where they need more support. Toward the end of the school year, or at the end of a curricular unit, it helps to look back at what you have asked them to do, carefully analyzing what worked and didn't work. Such reflection can reveal critical junctions where the curriculum or instruction made hidden demands on students, for which they may not have been developmentally ready. Either by yourself or in a group of teachers, you can use the following exercise as a starting point.

1. Look back at the year and select one substantial unit of study that went better than you hoped or expected.

Name of the unit: _____

Primary learning goals of the unit: _____

Your main instructional strategies: _____

_____

What did students enjoy most about the unit? _____

_____

What about its pacing seemed to work? _____

What learning risks in the classroom (trying new skills, asking questions, offering solutions) did students take during this unit? _____

In what ways did their learning go beyond what you intended for this curriculum unit? _____

_____

Were your students ready for this unit, in terms of:

Their background knowledge? _____

The nature of the unit's conceptual challenges? _____

The organization skills it required? _____

The collaboration skills it required? _____

Their interest in the material? _____

Were there any students for whom this unit did not work as well? If so, make notes here on that. _____

_____

How does thinking about student "readiness" help you understand their lack of success? _____

_____

2. Now think of a substantial unit of study for which the students' response disappointed you in some way.

Name of the unit: _____

Primary learning goals of the unit: _____

Your main instructional strategies: _____

_____

What about this unit did students like least? _____

What about the pacing did not work well for students? _____

What happened when the work of the unit required them to take learning risks in the classroom? _____

_____

How did they respond to the problems they encountered? _____

_____

Were your students "ready" for this unit, in terms of:

   Their background knowledge? _____

   The nature of the unit's conceptual challenges? _____

   The organization skills it required? _____

   The collaboration skills it required? _____

   Their interest in the material? _____

Were there any students for whom this unit worked well? If so, make notes here on that. _____

_____

How does thinking about student "readiness" help you understand their success? _____

_____

3. Based on these two examples from your curriculum, what might you do differently next year? _____

_____

Resources for Middle-Grades Teachers

UNDERSTANDING STUDENTS AND THEIR DEVELOPMENT

David Elkind, *All Grown Up and No Place to Go: Teenagers in Crisis* (New York: Perseus Books, 1998).

Mel Levine, *The Myth of Laziness* (New York: Simon & Schuster, 2003).

Michael J. Nakkula and Eric Toshalis, *Understanding Youth: Adolescent Development for Educators* (Cambridge, MA: Harvard Education Press, 2006).

Linda Perlstein, *Not Much Just Chillin': The Hidden Lives of Middle Schoolers* (New York: Farrar, Straus & Giroux, 2003).

Jeffrey J. Shultz and Alison Cook-Sather, *In Our Own Words: Students' Perspectives on School* (Lanham, MD: Rowman & Littlefield, 2001).

PRACTICAL ADVICE FOR MIDDLE-GRADES TEACHERS

Nancie Atwell, *In the Middle: New Understanding about Writing, Reading, and Learning* (Portsmouth, NH: Boynton/Cook, 1998).

Peter Johnston, *Choice Words: How Our Language Affects Children's Learning* (Portland, ME: Stenhouse Publishers, 2004).

Trudy Knowles and Dave F. Brown, *What Every Middle School Teacher Should Know* (Portsmouth, NH: Heinemann, 2000).

William J. Kreidler, *Conflict Resolution in the Middle School* (Cambridge, MA: Educators for Social Responsibility, 1997).

Paula Naegle, *The New Teachers Complete Sourcebook* (New York: Scholastic, 2002).

Rachel A. Poliner and Carol Miller Lieber, *The Advisory Guide: Designing and Implementing Effective Advisory Programs in Secondary Schools* (Cambridge, MA: Educators for Social Responsibility, 2004).

Sandra L. Schurr, *Dynamite in the Classroom: A How-To Book for Teachers* (Westerville, OH: National Middle School Association, 1994).

Cris Tovani, *I Read It, But I Don't Get It: Comprehension Strategies for Adolescent Readers* (Portland, ME: Stenhouse Publishers, 2000).

Harry Wong and Rosemary Wong, *The First Days of School: How to Be an Effective Teacher* (Mountain View, CA: Harry K. Wong Publications, 2004).

Rick Wormeli, *Meet Me in the Middle: Becoming an Accomplished Middle-Level Teacher* (Portland, ME: Stenhouse Publishers, 2001).

Rick Wormeli, *Day One and Beyond: Practical Matters for New Middle-Level Teachers* (Portland, ME: Stenhouse Publishers, 2003).

PERSPECTIVES ON SCHOOLING IN THE MIDDLE GRADES

Nancy Ames and Teri West, *Middle Level Curriculum, Instruction, and Assessment* (U.S. Department of Education, Office of Educational Research and Improvement, 1998).

James Beane, ed., *A Middle School Curriculum: From Rhetoric to Reality* (Westerville, OH: National Middle School Association, 1990).

Thomas O. Erb, ed., *This We Believe in Action: Implementing Successful Middle Level Schools* (Westerville, OH: National Middle School Association, 2005).

Anthony W. Jackson and P. Gayle Andrews, *Turning Points 2000: Educating Adolescents in the 21st Century* (New York: Teachers College Press, 2000).

Eric Jensen, *Teaching with the Brain in Mind* (Alexandria, VA: Association for Supervision and Curriculum Development, April 1998).

MetLife Survey of the American Teacher 2001: Key Elements of Quality Schools (New York: MetLife Foundation, 2001).

M. Hayes Mizell, *Shooting for the Sun: The Message of Middle School Reform* (New York: Edna McConnell Clark Foundation, 2002).

Nancy B. Mizelle, "Helping Middle School Students Make the Transition into High School," Digest No. EDO-PS-99–11 (Champaign, IL: ERIC Clearinghouse on Early Education and Parenting, August 1999).

Sandra Schurr, *Prescriptions for Success in Heterogeneous Classrooms* (Westerville, OH: National Middle School Association, 1995).

Theodore R. Sizer and Nancy Faust Sizer, *The Students Are Watching* (Boston: Beacon Press, 2000).

Anne Wheelock, *Safe to Be Smart: Building a Culture for Standards-Based Reform in the Middle Grades* (Westerville, OH: National Middle School Association, 1998).

Jon Wiles and Joseph C. Bondi, *The New American Middle School: Educating Preadolescents in an Era of Change*, 3rd ed. (Old Tappan, NJ: Prentice Hall, 2000).

BOOKS FOR MIDDLE-GRADES STUDENTS

Arlene Erlbach and Helen Flook, *The Middle School Survival Guide* (London: Walker Books, 2003).

Harriet Mosatche, *Too Old for This, Too Young for That! Your Survival Guide for the Middle-School Years* (Minneapolis, MN: Free Spirit Publishing, 2000).

BOOKS FOR PARENTS OF MIDDLE-GRADES STUDENTS

Kathleen Cushman, *What We Can't Tell You: Teenagers Talk to the Adults in Their Lives* (Providence, RI: Next Generation Press, 2005).

Anne Henderson, Karen Mapp, Vivian Johnson, and Don Davies, *Beyond the Bake Sale: The Essential Guide to Family-School Partnerships* (New York: The New Press, 2006).

Anthony W. Jackson and P. Gayle Andrews with Holly Holland and Priscilla Pardini, *Making the Most of Middle School: A Field Guide for Parents and Others* (New York: Teachers College Press, 2004).

ORGANIZATIONS AND WEBSITES

Association for Supervision and Curriculum Development (www.ascd.org) is a nonprofit organization that promotes student-centered teaching and learning across all grade levels. Its website offers a rich array of books and other publications, programs and professional development, and other stimulating materials of interest to teachers. The organization's magazine, *Educational Leadership*, published an especially helpful "Teaching the Tweens" issue in April 2006 (vol. 63, no. 7).

MiddleWeb: Exploring Middle School Reform (www.middleweb.com) is a website focusing exclusively on middle schools. It includes articles, research reports, email postings by teachers, and myriad other valuable links and information.

The National Forum to Accelerate Middle-Grades Reform (www.mgforum.org) is an alliance of over sixty educators, researchers, national associations, and officers of professional organizations and foundations committed to promoting the academic performance and healthy development of young adolescents. Its Schools to Watch program (www.schoolstowatch.org) highlights middle schools around the country that are notable for their responsiveness to early adolescent needs.

The National Middle School Association (www.nmsa.org) publishes journals, books, and other materials for educators and others on the education, growth, and development of young adolescents. It holds an annual fall conference.

Acknowledgments

Generous support for this project came from MetLife Foundation, as part of its commitment to strengthen the quality of education through improving communication among teachers, students, and communities. At The New Press, editor Ellen Reeves initiated the project, recognizing the need to pay special heed to the voices of younger adolescents. Barbara Cervone, president of What Kids Can Do, provided crucial support from inception to completion, both because WKCD sponsored the book's research and writing and because she contributed her own valuable advice throughout.

We owe particular thanks to the people and programs through which student contributors came to the project. Generous assistance and resources came from Rameka Blakey, co-director, and Mindy Weber, then co-director, at Providence Summerbridge, which is based at the Wheeler School in Providence, Rhode Island; from Meredith Laban, the director of Summerbridge San Francisco at University High School, and Samantha Johnson, who was then its dean of students; from Ricardo C. Morris, who was director of the Green Street Arts Center in Middletown, Connecticut; from the Youth Leadership Program of the

West 181st Street Neighborhood Project in New York City; and from Megan Howey, the Indiana project director of the Harmony/VISTA Service Learning Demonstration Project in Indianapolis, Indiana. Amy Goldbas and Bonnie Koba, at the Arts in Education division of the Connecticut Commission on Culture and Tourism, helped us connect with teachers in their Higher Order Thinking (HOT) Schools Summer Institute who gave valuable suggestions as we framed questions to ask our student contributors.

Each co-author of this book draws inspiration, support, and a perspective about adolescent development from the communities and organizations in which we work. For both of us, this includes the extended community of the Francis W. Parker Charter Essential School, a member of the Coalition of Essential Schools. Our abiding gratitude belongs to Theodore R. and Nancy Faust Sizer, whose spirit and hard work infused that school from its start.

The student-centered approach of Ted Sizer and Deborah Meier, and of the inspiring teachers and leaders of the Coalition of Essential Schools (CES) also influenced Kathleen Cushman, who wrote its journal *Horace* from 1989 to 2001 and now serves on its National Executive Board. When she co-founded the nonprofit What Kids Can Do (WKCD) with Barbara Cervone in 2001, that organization's emphasis on students' voices helped her gain a broader understanding of the issues of teaching and learning. Three very different daughters, Montana, Eliza, and Rosa Miller, also taught her a great deal over the past decades.

Laura Rogers first applied a developmental perspective to thorny adolescent issues under the guidance of Lawrence Kohlberg, Robert Selman, and Robert Kegan at the Harvard Graduate School of Education, and Donald Quinlan, at the Yale University School of Medicine. She continues the debates about adolescents and their learning (debates that never lead to simple answers) with her colleagues at the former Clinical Developmental Institute (Robert Kegan, Ann Fleck Henderson, Robert Goodman, Anne Colby, Betsy Speicher, Sharon Daloz Parks, Michael Basseches, and Gil Noam); with her students and colleagues at Tufts University; with Theresa Rogers and Robert Tierney, at the University of British Columbia; with William Damon, at Stanford University; and with Michael, Ben, and Molly Shear, at Laughing Stock Farm.

Perceptive comments from readers helped us enormously in the draft stages of our manuscript. For their thoughtful feedback on teaching and learning in the adolescent years we are especially grateful to Robert Kegan at the Harvard University Graduate School of Education; to Allison J. Kelaher Young, associate professor in the College of Education at Western Michigan University; to Tom Leyden, a former middle school principal now at the Texas Association of Secondary School Principals; to Laura Warner, a middle school teacher at the Parker School; and to Seewan Eng, now at WestEd, and Clare Ringwall, now the director of the New Teachers Collaborative at the Theodore R. Sizer Teachers Center, both of whom spent many years as teachers of the middle grades.

The intelligent help of editor Celia Bohannon was especially welcome in the early editorial stages, as we sorted through hundreds of pages of students' comments and reflections. Later, Jennifer Rappaport of The New Press provided timely guidance as the book moved through its production stages.

We are especially grateful for the steadfast friendship and support we received throughout, from each other and from those we hold most dear, as this book took shape.

The Student Contributors

The student contributors to this book came to us through the connections What Kids Can Do maintains with educators and youth development programs throughout the United States. These students all live in urban areas, and the schools they attended during the middle grades vary widely in description and configuration. Most are large district schools, but some are alternative public schools such as charter schools or district pilot schools, and a few are independent or parochial schools. School configurations also varied, with most serving either grades 6 through 8 or kindergarten through 8.

In Providence, Rhode Island, we worked with seventh and eighth graders involved in Providence Summerbridge, a Breakthrough Collaborative program that supports urban students in challenging academic programs from middle school through high school. In Middletown, Connecticut, our middle-grades contributors came from Green Street Arts, an after-school program providing enrichment to students and families in a low-income neighborhood. In San Francisco, we worked with seventh and eighth graders in the Summerbridge San Francisco program at University High School. In Indianapolis, students from two central city high schools worked with us in the first weeks of ninth grade, to contribute their thoughts on the transition to high school. New York City students came through a neighborhood youth organization in the Washington Heights neighborhood.

With their parents' or guardians' permission, we introduce students below by first name and grade in school at the time of our work with them, which took place in 2005 and 2006.*

Alex, grade 9
(Indianapolis)

Alma, grade 7
(San Francisco)

Amanda N., grade 8
(Middletown)

Amanda S., grade 9
(Indianapolis)

Amelia, grade 8
(Providence)

No Photo Available

Anastasia, grade 7
(San Francisco)

* A surname's initial appears only when two students have the same first name.

Ashley, grade 9
(Indianapolis)

Brandon, grade 9
(Indianapolis)

Brian, grade 9
(Indianapolis)

Canek, grade 8
(San Francisco)

Carmela, grade 8
(San Francisco)

Chandyn, grade 9
(Indianapolis)

Chanté, grade 9
(Indianapolis)

Christopher, grade 9
(Indianapolis)

Daniel, grade 8
(San Francisco)

Daquan, grade 7
(Providence)

Denue, grade 8
(Providence)

Diana, grade 7
(New York)

Edward, grade 7
(San Francisco)

Eric F., grade 7
(Middletown)

Eric Q., grade 7
(Middletown)

Gabriel, grade 7
(San Francisco)

Genesis, grade 7
(Providence)

Geoffery, grade 9
(Indianapolis)

Heather, grade 9
(Indianapolis)

Itai, grade 7
(San Francisco)

Jason, grade 7
(Providence)

Javier, grade 7
(Providence)

Jessica, grade 7
(Providence)

Kaitlyn, grade 9
(Indianapolis)

Katelin, grade 7
(Middletown)

Keith, grade 8
(Middletown)

Kenson, grade 8
(Providence)

Nyesha, grade 9
(Indianapolis)

Rachell, grade 9
(Indianapolis)

Shaniece, grade 7
(Middletown)

Tatzi, grade 8
(Middletown)

Thea, grade 8
(Middletown)

Tiffany, grade 7
(New York)

Veronica, grade 9
(Indianapolis)

Index

ethnic bias
  perception of, by students,
    22–23
  in teacher interactions with
    students, 86–87
exercises for teachers
  on fairness, 82–84
  on grading, 121–22
  on remembering the middle-grades
    experience, 12–13
  on sending students out of class,
    96–97
  on student collaboration,
    74–75
  on understanding classroom
    norms, 81

fairness
  classroom norms to ensure, 88
  individual versus group,
    88–92
  teacher exercise about, 82–84
  teacher, student perceptions of,
    76–77
  and teacher treatment of students,
    85–87
favoritism
  and fairness, 85–86, 98–99
  and race, 86–87
feedback to students, 114–17

first day(s) of school
  establishing respect in, 45
  in ninth-grade transition,
    185–87
  student worries about, 30–33,
    34
  teacher help with transitions in,
    33–38
food
  cleaning up, 147–50
  eating, in classroom, 146–50
  as factor in student attention,
    145–46
friendships among students,
    16–23
  negative influence of, 80
  romantic tensions in, 69–70
  in transition to ninth grade,
    175–76, 185

games for learning, 136–39, 195
grades
  effect on students of, 116–20
  exercise for teachers on, 121–22
  in high school, student worries
    about, 177
  parent responses to, 120
groups, student social
  in middle grades, 20–23
  in ninth grade, 174–76

Also Available from The New Press

BEYOND THE BAKE SALE
The Essential Guide to Family-School Partnerships
Anne T. Henderson, Karen L. Mapp, Vivian R. Johnson, and Don Davies

Countless studies demonstrate that students with parents actively involved in their education at home and school are more likely to earn higher grades and test scores, enroll in higher-level programs, graduate from high school, and go on to post-secondary education. *Beyond the Bake Sale* shows how to form these essential partnerships and how to make them work.

978-1-56584-888-7 (pb)

BLACK TEACHERS ON TEACHING
Michele Foster

An oral history of black teachers that gives "valuable insight into a profession that for African Americans was second only to preaching" (*Booklist*).

978-1-56584-453-7 (pb)

THE CASE FOR MAKE BELIEVE
Saving Play in a Commercialized World
Susan Linn

In the nationally celebrated *Consuming Kids,* Susan Linn provided an unsparing look at modern childhood molded by commercialism. In her new book, *The Case for Make Believe,* Linn argues that while play is crucial to human development and children are born with an innate capacity for make-believe, the convergence of ubiquitous technology and unfettered commercialism actually prevents them from playing.

978-1-56584-970-9 (hc)

COMING OF AGE AROUND THE WORLD
A Multicultural Anthology
Edited by Faith Adiele and Mary Frosch

Twenty-four stories by renowned international authors chronicle the modern struggle for identity among young people around the globe.

978-1-59558-080-1 (pb)

Also Available from The New Press

COMING OF AGE IN AMERICA
A Multicultural Anthology
Edited by Mary Frosch with a foreword by Gary Soto

The acne and ecstasy of adolescence, a multicultural collection of short stories and fiction excerpts that *Library Journal* calls "wonderfully diverse from the standard fare," in a beautiful new edition.

978-1-56584-147-5 (pb)

CONSUMING KIDS
The Hostile Takeover of Childhood
Susan Linn

In this shocking exposé, Susan Linn takes a comprehensive and unsparing look at the demographic advertisers call "the kid market," taking readers on a compelling and disconcerting journey through modern childhood as envisioned by commercial interests.

978-1-56584-783-5 (hc)

EVERYDAY ANTIRACISM
Getting Real About Race in School
Edited by Mica Pollock

Which acts by educators are "racist" and which are "antiracist"? How can an educator constructively discuss complex issues of race with students and colleagues? In *Everyday Antiracism* leading educators deal with the most challenging questions about race in school, offering invaluable and effective advice.

978-1-59558-054-2 (pb)

FIRES IN THE BATHROOM
Advice to Teachers from High School Students
Kathleen Cushman

This groundbreaking book offers original insights into teaching teenagers in today's hard-pressed urban high schools from the point of view of the students themselves. It speaks to both new and established teachers, giving them first-hand information about who their students are and what they need to succeed.

978-1-56584-996-9 (pb)

Also Available from The New Press

GROWING UP GAY/GROWING UP LESBIAN
A Literary Anthology
Edited by Bennett L. Singer

The first literary anthology geared specifically to gay and lesbian youth. *A Library Journal* Notable Book of the Year.

978-1-56584-103-1 (pb)

HELP WANTED
Tales from the First Job Front
Sydney Lewis

"A protégé of legendary oral historian Studs Terkel, Lewis astutely allows twenty-somethings to tell their stories in their own words."—*Publishers Weekly*

978-1-56584-745-3 (pb)

MAY IT PLEASE THE COURT
Courts, Kids, and the Constitution
Edited by Peter Irons

Sixteen Supreme Court cases on the constitutional rights of teachers and students involving school prayer, library censorship, political protest, and corporal punishment.

978-1-56584-613-5 (boxed set: hc with 4 cassettes)

THE NEW PRESS EDUCATION READER
Leading Educators Speak Out
Edited by Ellen Gordon Reeves

The New Press Education Reader brings together the work of progressive writers and educators—among them Lisa Delpit, Herbert Kohl, William Ayers, and Maxine Greene—to discuss the most pressing and challenging issues now facing us, including schools and social justice, equity issues, tracking and testing, combating racism and homophobia, and more.

978-1-59558-110-5 (pb)

Also Available from The New Press

OTHER PEOPLE'S CHILDREN
Cultural Conflict in the Classroom
Lisa Delpit

In this anniversary edition of a classic, MacArthur Award-winning author Lisa Delpit develops ideas about ways teachers can be better "cultural transmitters" in the classroom, where prejudice, stereotypes, and cultural assumptions breed ineffective education.

978-1-59558-074-0 (pb)

TEACHERS HAVE IT EASY
The Big Sacrifices and Small Salaries of America's Teachers
Daniel Moulthrop, Nínive Clements Calegari, and Dave Eggers

The bestselling call to action for improving the working lives of public school teachers—and improving our classrooms along the way.

978-1-59558-128-0 (pb)

"A TOTALLY ALIEN LIFE FORM"
Teenagers
Sydney Lewis

More than fifty teens are interviewed and talk candidly about sex in the age of AIDS, violence at home and on the street, politics, race relations, education, and religion.

978-1-56584-283-0 (pb)

THE WORLD OUT THERE
Becoming Part of the Lesbian and Gay Community
Michael Thomas Ford

A no-nonsense introduction aimed at young adults that provides useful advice on dating, AIDS, and coping with being different.

978-1-56584-234-2 (pb)